# *The* DEMIVEG COOKBOOK

# The
# DEMIVEG
## COOKBOOK
### David Scott

BLOOMSBURY

First published in Great Britain 1987
Copyright © 1987 by David Scott

Bloomsbury Publishing Ltd, 2 Soho Square, London W1

British Library Cataloguing in Publication Data
Scott, David, 1944-
The demiveg cookbook
1. Cookery (Natural foods)
I. Title
641.5′637    TX741

ISBN 0–7475–0053–3

Designed by Fielding Rowinski
Illustrated by George Hardie
Photography by Charlie Stebbings
Food prepared by Nigel Slater
Styled by Totty Whately
Phototypeset by Falcon Graphic Art Ltd, Wallington, Surrey
Printed and bound in Great Britain by Butler & Tanner Ltd, Frome, Somerset

# CONTENTS

*Acknowledgements*

I would like to thank Jules Shield at La Grande Bouffe
restaurant, Liverpool, for the twenty practical and imaginative recipes
she contributed to this book, and my long-time partner in the
Everyman Bistro Paddy Byrne, who knows as much about food and
cookery as anyone I have met, for the chapter Fruit For Dessert.
Special thanks to all at Bloomsbury Publishing, particularly Jane Carr
and David Reynolds and to my copy editor Sue Hogg.

The publishers would like to thank David Mellor Design Ltd (4 Sloane
Square, London SW1W 8EE; 26 James Street, Covent Garden,
London WC3E 8PA; 66 King Street, Manchester M2 4NP) for the
kind loan of accessories.

# INTRODUCTION

A demivegetarian is someone who cares about good food and healthy eating and who enjoys a mixed diet of vegetarian foods, fish and chicken. For health and/or humane reasons demivegetarians do not eat red meat or pork. At the same time, for practical or personal reasons they are not vegetarians. This may be because they need to cater for a family with mixed views about vegetarianism or because of the difficulties total vegetarians often encounter in trying to maintain a balanced diet when travelling or eating out in restaurants or with friends. Demivegetarianism also appeals to those whose metabolism is ill-suited to diets that contain too much flesh food or, indeed, not enough.

The intention of this book is to provide a collection of exciting and practical recipes plus the nutritional and culinary information required to allow the user to plan interesting and delicious meals which reflect their own culinary tastes, nutritional needs and attitude towards diet. It is essentially divided into three sections: nutrition, cook's notes and recipes.

The nutrition chapter discusses the book's dietary goals and comments on essential nutrients, the do's and don'ts of a good demivegetarian diet, how to shape your diet to suit your individual needs, healthy snacks, and menu planning based on demivegetarianism.

The cook's notes include information on the purchasing, preparation, culinary uses and choice of vegetables and fruits, grains and beans, fish, poultry and dairy products. There are also suggestions on kitchen equipment, details of ingredients which may be unfamiliar to the reader and advice on stocking a demivegetarian pantry.

The recipes in the main section of the book are divided equally into the following categories: starters; soups; salads and dressings; vegetables and sauces; fish; chicken; grains and pasta; beans and beancurd; fruit for dessert.

The recipes have been chosen to provide tasty, uncomplicated and colourful dishes that can contribute to a light, energy-giving, nutritionally balanced diet. The sources of the recipes are wide and various, but my own interest in Middle and Far Eastern cooking gives the selection a certain flavour.

Finally, the word 'demivegetarian' is new but the idea behind it is not. If one looks at what is judged to be a desirable and healthy way of eating by traditional cooks in various cultures around the world it is a demivegetarian diet which emerges. For instance, a traditional Japanese meal of rice, beancurd (tofu), pickles and fish; the Mexican peasant meal of re-fried beans, cornmeal tortillas, cheese or meat, lettuce, tomatoes and onions; or the Middle Eastern street food of pitta bread stuffed with chickpea rissoles, raw vegetables and yoghourt. Grains and vegetables are considered primary foods, with fish, poultry, legumes, fruit and dairy products (or soyabean products in the East) playing essential supporting roles. This combination of foodstuffs has even been called the 'universal diet' (see *Diet and Nutrition: A Holistic Approach* by Rudolph Ballentine MD, published by the Himalayan International Institute, Pennsylvania).

# NUTRITION

The ideal demivegetarian diet is one which gives gastronomic pleasure and promotes optimum health. It is composed of foods prepared from plants, fish, chicken and dairy produce, grown or reared in as natural an environment as possible. They should be eaten fresh or, at second best, deep frozen. Some processed foods are unavoidable, but we should choose those which have had fewest nutrients removed and the fewest chemicals added (including synthetic vitamins). For example, 100 per cent wholewheat stoneground flour is a processed flour but nothing edible or nutritional has been removed and nothing has been added. On the other hand, in the production of white flour important nutrients are removed and synthetic chemicals are added. Nowadays some manufacturers put back certain of the vitamins and minerals they have removed into the flour, but in different proportions from those that occur naturally and without the trace elements which are found in the whole grain. Other examples of foods which are processed but which retain their goodness are honey (as opposed to white sugar) and

cold-pressed vegetable oils (as opposed to hot-pressed and hydrogenated fats).

The combination of foods we eat and their relative quantities are also important in a good demivegetarian diet. We need to ensure that we have satisfactory amounts of proteins, carbohydrates, vitamins, minerals, fibre and fat, and that we maintain a balance between what we eat and the energy we expend. Otherwise we get too thin or too fat. Whole grains such as brown rice, oats, millet and wholewheat are nature's perfect foods because the balance of nutrients they contain are most suited to our needs. Eaten in combination with vegetables and fruit, they make a major contribution to a balanced diet. If, alongside these two food groups, we include in our diet small amounts of chicken and fish, beans, seeds and nuts, eggs, milk, yoghourt and cheese, it will contain all the nutrients we require in satisfactory quantities and in the right combinations.

The seven main food groups in the demivegetarian diet and the approximate contribution they should make to the diet are as follows:

| | |
|---|---|
| Whole grains and grain products (bread, pasta and so on) | 30-35% |
| Fresh vegetables and fruit, cooked and raw | 20-25% |
| Beans, nuts and seeds | 10-15% |
| Eggs, milk, cheese, yoghourt | 10-15% |
| Fish and chicken | 10-15% |
| Vegetable fats (preferably unsaturated) | 2.5% |
| Sweeteners, spices, salt, herbs, vinegars | 2.5% |

## *Proteins, Carbohydrates, Fats, Vitamins, Minerals and Fibre*

For the growth, maintenance, energy, repair and regulation of metabolic processes the body needs proteins, carbohydrates, fats, vitamins and minerals. For a healthy and energy-giving diet all five groups are needed in the right balance. Proteins are necessary for the growth, repair and maintenance of bodily tissues. Carbohydrates and fats provide energy for the body's activities, and fats are also the source of the fat-soluble vitamins A, D, E and K. Vitamins and minerals are required in very small amounts but they are essential for the right functioning and the regulation of all the body's processes. Fibre is essential for the efficient elimination of waste products.

### *Protein*

A worry for some people when they exclude red meat from their diets is that they will not get enough protein. There is no need for this concern because a mixed demivegetarian diet provides sufficient protein for all a normal adult's and child's needs. Fish and chicken are rich in protein, and plant foods such as grains and beans are also good sources, particularly if eaten in combination with each other (see below). Dairy products such as milk, cheese and eggs are another protein source, although, as with red meats, they may contain a lot of saturated fats. For this reason, eat them in moderation and, where possible, buy a proportion of low-fat products such as skimmed milk or cottage cheese.

### Protein complementarity

Although plant foods such as grains and beans are good sources of protein, many of them lack one or more of the essential amino acids which, if present, would give them a very high protein value. Fortunately, the amino acid in short supply in one plant food is often available in excess in another and vice versa. By combining two or more complementary plant foods in one meal we obtain protein of much higher quality and biological value. For example, most grains (such as rice, wheat and corn) and grain products are high in the amino acid tryptophan but low in lysine, while most pulses (such as beans, peas and lentils) are high in lysine and low in tryptophan. Thus a dish containing, say, rice *and* lentils will supply protein of a higher biological value than the same total weight of rice or lentils on their own.

The food groups which complement one another's individual biological values are grains, beans, nuts and seeds eaten in combination with one another or individually with dairy products, chicken or fish.

### Carbohydrates

Carbohydrates are the body's main source of energy. They are present in foods as starches and sugars. Starch is obtained from cereal grains and their products, pulses, vegetables (especially root vegetables) and nuts. The combination of starches and protein in these foods is a good one for people involved in manual work or sporting effort. Naturally occurring sugars are found in fruit, honey and milk. Refined sugar, added liberally to so many foods, should be used moderately. It lacks every nutrient except carbohydrate and by spoiling the appetite it tends to displace other foods containing the nutrients we need from our diet.

### Fats

Fats provide a concentrated energy source and the essential fat-soluble vitamins A, D and E. Every fat or oil contains active (unsaturated) or inactive (saturated) acids, or both. Very simply, active acids react positively with other nutrients in the bloodstream, while inactive acids do not react and may clog up the system. The active acids are called essential fatty acids (EFA). They are contained in the polyunsaturated fats recommended by many authorities in preference to saturated fats as a precaution against heart disease. The saturated fats generally come from animal sources such as red meats, butter, cream and cheese. Thus, where there is a choice, use vegetable oils such as sunflower seed, olive, safflower and sesame seed oils, polyunsaturated margarines and low-fat cheeses or other low-fat milk products in your cooking. I would also recommend that fats of any description be used in only moderate amounts, particularly saturated fats. There is now a considerable body of opinion to support the claim that the risk of heart disease, high blood pressure and some cancers can be reduced by cutting saturated-fat intake.

### Vitamins and minerals

The body cannot synthesize the vitamins and minerals it requires and they must be supplied in the food we eat. The vitamins and minerals are all distinct substances, unrelated to each other, but their functions in the body *are* interrelated and they are all required in the right balance. A mixed diet of whole grains, pulses, dairy products, vegetables, including salads and fresh fruit, plus small amounts of chicken and fish, will normally provide all the vitamins and minerals we need.

### Fibre

Fibre is found in unrefined cereals, fruit and vegetables. It has no nutritional value because it is not digested, but because it adds bulk to the body's waste products it is essential for their efficient elimination.

The nutrients each of the food groups best provides are as follows:

*Protein:* whole grains, fish, chicken, beans, nuts, seeds, dairy products and, in small amounts, but of high quality, from green vegetables

*Complex carbohydrates:* whole grains, fresh fruit and vegetables

*Vitamins and minerals:* unrefined fresh foods of all types

*Fibre:* whole grains, fresh fruit and vegetables

*Fats:* unhydrogenated vegetable oils; where available, cold-pressed oils are the best

## The Do's and Don'ts of a Good Demivegetarian Diet

### Do's

1 Eat lots of vegetables and fresh fruit each day. Include at least one salad a day with your meals.
2 Ensure whole grains in the form of wholemeal bread, wholemeal pasta, brown rice or other cooked grains and breakfast cereals form part of your staple diet.
3 Substitute poultry or fish for red meat. Eat fish or chicken at least twice a week but not at each main meal.
4 Use skimmed milk and low-fat dairy products, polyunsaturated margarines, and vegetable oils such as olive oil, sunflower oil and corn oil. Remember, however, only to eat moderate amounts of any fats and oils.
5 Eat a wide selection of different foods.
6 Buy good-quality, fresh vegetables and fruit and, when possible, buy them in season.
7 Buy the freshest fish you can find. Use frozen fish only as a convenience.
8 It's a tall order, but ask your poultry supplier for the best and most humanely reared chicken he can obtain. The more pressure created by the general public, the sooner free-range, organically fed chickens will be generally available.
9 Dilute fruit juice. The neat variety from the carton is too concentrated for most people to digest easily.

If as a general rule you follow the above suggestions, then there is no reason not to include occasionally in your diet refined foods such as white sugar, white rice and white bread and sometimes to eat butter and cream cakes – but, remember, moderation is the word. On that basis, if, for instance, you prefer white rice to brown rice, then eat white rice, but make sure you compensate for this by eating other whole grains, wholemeal bread and wholemeal pasta.

## Don'ts

1 Don't eat too many processed foods.
2 Don't eat foods that contain a lot of artificial flavourings and colourings.
3 Don't overcook vegetables.
4 Don't eat too much salt.
5 Don't eat too many snacks such as biscuits, cakes, pastries, ice cream, roasted and salted peanuts, crisps.
6 Don't eat sugared breakfast cereals, soft drinks and squashes, chocolates and other sweets.
7 Don't eat hardened margarine or those made from synthetically produced fats.
8 Don't overeat or miss meals because you are too busy.
9 Don't eat when you are agitated or angry.
10 Don't consume too much alcohol with a meal. One or two glasses is enough.
11 Don't drink too much coffee.

### The Demivegetarian diet and weight loss

A diet of whole grains, fresh vegetables and fruit, augmented by beans, seeds and nuts, fish, chicken and dairy products, together with a lifestyle that includes regular exercise, is, for most people, enough to ensure weight loss if the regime is new, or to maintain a steady healthy weight if it is already a well-established way of life.

## Keeping Fit

If you start exercising regularly you may discover that you do not need to be so careful about what you eat because you will not put on weight so easily. At the same time, because exercise makes you more aware of your body's needs, you may, paradoxically, decide to take more care over your diet. The workings of the body are complex, and nutrition is a controversial subject, but two facts about diet are quite clear. First, for an overweight but otherwise healthy person, exercise is a more efficient and longer lasting way of losing weight than dieting. Secondly, the fitter we are and the more in tune with our bodies we are, the more care we will take over our diets. The effects of overdrinking, smoking and too much junk food will be experienced more severely and more quickly by the fit person than the unfit. This is one reason, of course, why some people choose to stay unfit. Alternatively, if you choose to stay fit and eat sensibly, then you are more likely to be healthy, to enjoy a sense of well-being, to have more energy and to live longer.

## *Individualizing your diet*

To consider food in terms of nutrition as opposed to those of cuisine (which describe a style of cooking) is to consider it from the point of view of its effect on our health and sense of well-being. Decisions about diet are thus highly personal ones and each of us is our own best judge of what is the right diet for ourselves. If what we eat keeps us in good health and gives us the energy to do what we want to do, then it is the right one for our needs.

The basic guideline for discovering our own needs is the exercise of moderation and awareness. Initially, it is difficult to listen to the body, but if we slowly start to take note and act upon messages such as 'I've had enough', 'I should eat', 'I should eat more slowly', 'I need more fresh food', then we get more attuned to our bodies' needs.

The starting point for balanced eating based on a demivegetarian diet should be a varied diet of natural foods composed of whole grains or whole grain products, fresh vegetables and fruit, fish, poultry, beans, unhydrogenated vegetable oils, nuts, seeds and dairy products. Natural foods taste better than refined foods and their nutrient and fibre content is always higher. A diet composed mainly of refined foods, often full of sugar and additives, saturated fats and too much salt is definitely bad for health.

Once a reasonably good diet has been established, we can carry out some fine tuning. There are three basic metabolic body types. First, there are those suited to an 'alkalinizing' diet in which proteins should be obtained from mainly vegetarian sources, poultry and fish, which are only moderately acid-forming, but not from red meat, which is highly acid-forming. They are called 'sympathetics' in nutritional parlance. Secondly, there are those suited to an 'acidifying' diet in which red meat should make an important dietary contribution. Such people are called 'parasympathetics'. Thirdly, there are those suited to a mixed diet. Within these three groups there are many variations, but the great majority of people belong to the first or third groups. Even within the second group there is a leaning towards a mixed diet rather than a rich red-meat one.

A basic demivegetarian diet (or 'mixed diet' in the above terminology) is thus highly suitable as a benchmark for discovering which diet is best-suited to our own metabolic type. By increasing or reducing the various components in our diet, we can discover the balance that best matches our requirements. Remember, however, that these requirements may change with age, vocation, life style, environment, emotional life and so on, and, in fact, keeping to the right diet is a never-ending process of awareness and change.

The chart below lists the foods most suited to alkaline, sympathetic (vegetarian-biased) metabolisms, those most suited to acid, parasympathetic (meat-rich) metabolisms and those foods that are neutral. Everybody needs a combination of all three but, as explained, some of us are better suited to eating more of some of the foods in one group than the others. Discovering our own balance is a question of experiment. For instance, if you are basically a sympathetic type, then a dinner of steak will make you feel lethargic, while foods such as grains, nuts and cheese will pick you up. Mixed types will enjoy vegetable proteins and fish and poultry dishes and feel good after them. Parasympathetics enjoy nothing more than a joint of meat and feel full of energy after eating one.

| Alkaline foods | Neutral foods | Acid foods |
|---|---|---|
| Vegetables | Vegetable oils | Meat |
| Fruit (except plums and cranberries, which are acid)* | Honey | Poultry |
| | Sugar | Fish |
| | Butter, milk and cream | Eggs |
| Salt, herbs, spices and soya sauce | | Cheese |
| Tea and coffee | | Grains and grain products (except millet, which is alkaline) |
| Wine and mineral water | | Beans |
| | | Nuts |
| | | Food additives |
| | | Beer |

* The acids in fruit are converted by the body into carbon dioxide, water and a mineral ash which has an alkaline effect on the system.

## Healthy snacks

Snack foods in particular are often too sweet, too fatty or too salty and they are sometimes rightly described as 'junk food'. Where possible, avoid the popular commercial snacks and substitute natural foods. They taste better and have much higher nutrient and fibre content. One word of caution: many manufacturers, aware that whole foods are now more popular, tag the words 'healthy', 'whole' or 'wholesome' onto unhealthy, unwholesome products, so look at the ingredients carefully.

Fresh fruit is the most obvious healthy snack food. Fruit in season, thoroughly washed, is usually the best-tasting and cheapest. Dried fruit such as apricots, figs, bananas and dates is also convenient. Nuts, singly or mixed, preferably unsalted, are nutritious and filling. Many wholefood and health shops now sell snack mixes such as trail mix, Bombay mix and tropical fruit mix. These are usually good, especially if mixed and packed in the shop. Wholemeal bread with cheese and green salad is an excellent snack. Muesli with fruit and yoghourt is not just a breakfast food – it can quickly and healthily fill a mid-morning or mid-afternoon gap.

## Menu Planning

The skeleton menus suggested below are based on balanced combinations of the six food groups we have already identified. They provide meals for a normal balanced metabolism but can be adjusted to suit particular needs. For instance, men and women newly concerned with improving their diets by excluding red meats may initially use more fish

15

and chicken recipes than vegetarian ones. On the other hand, long-term vegetarians who are slowly changing to a demivegetarian-style diet may begin by choosing more vegetarian dishes. Or, in either case, if they have guests coming to dinner who normally eat a different diet from themselves, they can choose a menu that is primarily vegetarian or vice versa.

### Menu Structure (Main Meal of the Day)

| Days 1 and 4 | Day 2 | Day 3 (and maybe 7) |
|:---:|:---:|:---:|
| Whole grains | Whole grains | Whole grains |
| Vegetables | Vegetables | Vegetables |
| Beans and seeds | Dairy produce | Fish or poultry |

| Day 5 (and maybe 7) | | Day 6 |
|:---:|:---:|:---:|
| Whole grains | | Whole grains |
| Fish or poultry | | Fish or poultry |
| Beans, nuts, seeds | | Beans, nuts, seeds |
| Vegetables | | Dairy produce |
| | | Vegetables |

Fruit to be eaten with any meal.

The specific dishes may, of course, be selected from recipes which make up this book.

# COOK'S NOTES

I n this chapter you will find information on the purchasing, preparation and varieties of foods available in each of the following demivegetarian food groups: vegetables and fruit; grains, beans, nuts and seeds; poultry and fish; eggs, cheese and yoghurt. Basic kitchen equipment, usual ingredients and the stocking of a demivegetarian pantry are also discussed.

## *Vegetables and Fruit*

One of the essentials of good cooking and healthy eating is to choose ingredients at their best. This is particularly the case with fruit and vegetables. To ensure that fruit and vegetables are of the highest quality, buy in season and select produce from farms and orchards as close to home as possible. In this way you will be buying them at their freshest and cheapest. Remember also to take particular advantage of the flavoursome short-season crops such as soft fruit and asparagus. Shopping for basics in this manner then gives you more freedom

occasionally to buy and enjoy some of the wide range of exotic fruit and vegetables now being imported into Britain.

Always wash vegetables thoroughly and, where suitable, give them a good scrub. Peel them only if strictly necessary because the skin contains many nutrients and is often tasty. As a basic rule, cook vegetables in the minimum of time and water necessary. The aim is always to ensure that they retain their colour and texture. If you can find a supply of pesticide-free, organically grown vegetables, do make use of it. If you cannot, ask your local greengrocer to start stocking them. The bigger the demand, the more likely our farmers will be to take note.

### Seasonal buying

Below are general details of which fruit and vegetables, both home-grown and imported, are particularly worth looking out for in each season. The lists are by no means comprehensive and do not include items generally available all year round such as mushrooms and beansprouts. They are a guide to good buys, but note that these will change in time as export and import markets change.

*Spring:* asparagus, avocados, baby white turnips, bananas, calabrese, chicory, citrus fruit, cucumbers, curly endive, courgettes, green beans, mangetout peas, mint, new potatoes, parsley, pineapples, radishes, spinach beet, tomatoes, watercress

*Summer:* apples, aubergines, beetroot, beans, broccoli, carrots, cauliflower, celery, corn on the cob, courgettes, fennel, French beans, garlic, globe artichokes, kidney beans, lettuce (all types), peppers, plum-tomatoes, runner beans, Spanish onions, tomatoes, watercress

*Autumn:* apples, avocados, basil, cabbage (drumhead), celery, chicory, chillies, Chinese cabbage, courgettes, cucumbers, fresh dates, endive, fennel, flageolet beans, French beans, grapes, kiwi fruit, pomegranates, red peppers, root crops (all types), runner beans, shallots, spinach, sweetcorn, tomatoes, watercress

*Winter:* avocados, beetroot, broccoli (purple and white), cabbage (red and white), carrots, calabrese, cauliflower, celery, chicory, coriander, courgettes, endive, French beans, leeks, lemons, lettuce (iceberg or cos), mangetout peas, new potatoes, oranges, parsley, potatoes

### How best to cook your fruit and vegetables

*Root Vegetables:* Carrots, potatoes and the like are best cooked at a fast simmer/slow boil. You want to cook the vegetables swiftly to retain as much flavour as possible, but you do not want to have the heat so high that the water is violently agitated, causing the outer parts of the vegetables to disintegrate before the centre is cooked.

For the best results, place the root vegetables in three times their volume of cold water, place the lid on the pan and bring swiftly to the boil, then reduce the heat and cook until tender.

### Green vegetables

Green beans, broccoli and other green vegetables are exceptional in that they are best cooked in an open pan at a furious boil. The reason is this: these vegetables contain substances which, under the action of heat, act to change the vegetable from bright green to a cheerless khaki colour. Fortunately the chemicals are volatile and if you can drive them off and out of the pan before they have a chance to act, your vegetables will remain green. You must then serve them immediately, or, if they are for a salad, chill them under a cold tap or plunge them into iced water until they are quite cold.

When cooking in this manner note the following points:

1  The vegetables are normally cooked in salted water because the salt raises the temperature of boiling water a little, allowing the offending substances to be driven off a little more efficiently.
2  Have only ½-¾ in water in your pan. There should not be enough water in the pan for the vegetables to charge around and break up.
3  Have the water at a furious boil before you put in the green vegetables and keep it boiling.
4  Use a large-based pan and do not overcrowd. It will not matter if parts of the vegetables protrude, but they must be in close proximity to the boiling water.

### Tender-leaf vegetables

Vegetables such as spinach should be washed well, the excess water shaken off, and cooked without any additional water over a moderate heat in a covered pan.

### Fruit

Fruit is traditionally poached in a sugar syrup. The slow cooking prevents the fruit from breaking up, and the strong sugar solution prevents the flavour and the natural sugars from leaking away, as would happen if the fruit was cooked in water. Poaching the fruit in syrup may preserve the flavour, but it causes you to consume hefty doses of sugar.

You should, whenever possible, try to eat much of your fruit raw in order to take full advantage of its abundant vitamin C. If you cook it, keep the cooking to a minimum, again to retain as much of the vitamin C as possible. Rather than stewing fruit in even the minimum of water, try baking it or steaming it whole in its skin. For example, wash pears well and place them complete in a steamer basket. Cook them until just soft, allow them to cool, peel them with a sharp knife, slice them in half and remove the core with a teaspoon. Stuff the pear halves or cut them into segments.

### Dried fruit

Dried fruit is a very useful ingredient in the demivegetarian diet. As long as you remember to soak those that need it ahead of time, dried fruit is an excellent ready-to-use ingredient in muesli and other breakfast cereals, in dried- and fresh-fruit salads, in savoury stuffings, casseroles, rice dishes, soups and sauces. Dried fruit is nourishing and versatile and contains all the goodness of fresh fruit in a concentrated form. Dried fruit is generally rich in vitamins, minerals and energy-giving sugars (which are much less damaging to teeth than ordinary refined sugar) and also contains small amounts of protein.

Traditionally, the fruit most often dried are dates, grapes (as raisins, currants and sultanas), figs, plums (as prunes) and apricots. More recently dried apples, bananas, pears and even peaches have become popular. The whole range of dried fruit, either individually or in mixed bags, is available in health-food stores and better supermarkets. Where there is a choice, buy the sun-dried varieties (or, second best, freeze-dried) rather than those dried by artificial heating, a process which kills vitamin C. Dried fruits will keep for up to a year, or for even longer deep-frozen. They are often considerably cheaper if bought in bulk, and if you have storage space this is the most economical way to purchase them.

### Raw vegetables and fruit

Raw fruit contains nutrients and fibre, and many studies have been published in recent years which confirm the valuable contribution that salads and fresh fruit make to a healthy diet and to the prevention of disease. It is therefore a good idea to eat at least one salad and some fresh fruit each day.

### Vegetable and fruit juices

Raw fruit and vegetable juices provide an excellent way of obtaining the nutrients of fruit and vegetables in a quick, convenient and concentrated form. Juices are rich in vitamins, minerals, enzymes and natural sugars, and are easily assimilated into the bloodstream. Carrot and celery juice are good staple ingredients and they are useful for combining with other, stronger-tasting vegetable juices which are not very appetizing on their own. Pineapples, pears and apples serve the same role in the preparation of fruit juices. Among many others, the following juice combinations are both nutritious and tasty: carrot and apple; carrot and tomato; carrot and celery; orange and pineapple; papaya and pineapple; orange and grapefruit; carrot, apple and lettuce (in 5:3:1 proportions).

# Grains

Grains are the edible seeds of cereal grains. They are literally embryonic plants and as such are small packages of nourishment and energy. Grains provide the world with its principal food source. They contain protein, carbohydrates, vitamins, minerals and fibre in excellent proportions for our needs. The main grains we eat in the West are rice, wheat (mainly as flour in bread and pasta and so on, but also as bulgar wheat and couscous), barley, oats, millet and buckwheat.

Purchase grains from a reputable and busy health- or wholefood store to ensure they have not been kept for an overlong period. At home, store grains in airtight containers in a cool, dry place. If possible, buy organically grown grains and ensure that they are whole and unrefined.

All grains are very good cooked on their own in water and then served as a side dish to vegetables or with a sauce, or combined with raw vegetables and made into a salad. Cooked grains can also be mixed with other ingredients and baked or used to stuff vegetables or make rissoles. Some grains benefit from dry-roasting before being boiled in water. This is particularly the case with buckwheat (kasha).

To dry-roast or toast grains, heat the grains, with stirring and shaking, in a dry frying pan or saucepan over a moderate heat until they gently brown.

The general rules for cooking grains are as follows. Rinse the grain under the cold-water tap and drain. Measure the cooking water into the pot and bring it to the boil.

Add the grain, stir, add salt if you wish (¼-½ teaspoon per 8 oz/225 g grain), return the pot to the boil. Reduce the heat to very low. Cover the pot and cook until the grain is tender and the water has been absorbed. Cooking times, water-to-grain ratios and other tips are given in the table below.

| Grain | Water:grain ratio | Cooking time |
|---|---|---|
| Barley (whole) | 3:1 | 1 hour |
| Buckwheat | 2:1 | 15-20 minutes |
| Bulgar wheat | 2:1 | 15-20 minutes |
| Millet | 3:1 | 40-45 minutes |
| Rice – white | 1½ to 2:1 | 15-20 minutes |
| – brown | 2:1 | 50-60 minutes |
| Wholewheat berries | 3:1 | 1½-2 hours |
| Cracked wheat | 2:1 | 15-20 minutes |
| Wild rice | 3:1 | 1 hour |

### Cooking tips

1 8 oz (225 g) uncooked grains gives about 1½ lb (700 g) cooked grains.
2 1 volume uncooked grains gives about 3 volumes cooked grains.
3 3 oz (75 g) uncooked grains per person is an average serving.
4 Do not stir grains during cooking – it makes them sticky.
5 For a change, sauté the grains with some chopped onion in a little oil before adding the cooking water – it changes their flavour.
6 Cook whole lentils and brown rice together sometimes for variety.
7 Combine leftover grains and beans, add a dressing and chopped salad vegetables and serve as a salad.
8 Add herbs or spices to the cooking water.
9 Sprinkle cooked grains with roasted nuts or seeds.
10 Replace the cooking water with stock.

# Beans

'Beans' is the term generally used to describe the seeds of the plants of the legume family, which includes beans, peas and lentils. Baked and cooked properly, they are a versatile, tasty, economical and nutritious food. Beans are particularly good sources of the B vitamins thiamine and niacin, and the minerals calcium and iron. Sprouted beans are also high in vitamin C.

Beans contain two starches which are difficult to digest if they are not broken down before eating. For this reason it is essential that they are soaked and cooked for the correct time before consumption. This particularly applies to kidney beans, which also contain a harmful substance destroyed only by correct cooking.

Store beans in a dry, cool place in airtight containers. They come in many fascinating and attractive shapes and colours, so, if you can, store them in glass containers on open shelves. Before cooking, check the beans for any small stones or grit. This is especially necessary with lentils.

Nearly all the beans and peas must be soaked for a long time before cooking to ensure that they are digestible. This means that you need to remember to put the beans in to soak well in advance of the meal. The usual soaking time is twelve to twenty-four hours, although there is a quicker method which is discussed below. Strictly speaking, lentils and split peas do not require soaking, but soaking does not do them any harm and speeds up the cooking time.

### Standard soaking method

Weigh out the beans you require (8 oz/225 g serves about four people) and pick them over to remove any grit or stones or odd-looking beans. Cover the beans in cold water (2 pints/1.1 litre per 8 oz/225 g beans). Leave according to the recommended soaking times given in the chart below. If the beans are to be cooked in the water they were soaked in, by the end of the cooking time the water will be almost completely absorbed and the beans will not need to be drained. This method preserves any vitamins otherwise lost in the water. Of course, more water may be added during cooking as necessary. If you forget or need to leave the beans longer than the recommended soaking time, then they should be drained and covered with fresh water before cooking.

### Quick soaking method

If you forget to put the beans on to soak, here is a quick cooking method. Place the beans in a heavy saucepan and cover them with water as directed in the standard soaking method. Cover the pot and bring to the boil, reduce the heat and simmer for 5 minutes. Now remove the pot from the heat and leave the beans to soak for the quick-method time given in the chart below. Then bring the beans to the boil in the same water and cook until tender. Cooking times are the same as for the standard-soaking method.

### Pressure cooking

Pressure cooking tends to reduce the flavour of beans and make them mushy. I recommend it only if you are in a rush. Times are given in the chart below.

22

▼▼▼▼▼▼▼▼▼▼▼▼▼▼▼▼▼▼▼▼▼▼▼▼▼▼▼▼▼▼▼▼▼

# Soaking and Cooking Times

| Beans | Soaking times (hours) | | Cooking times | |
|---|---|---|---|---|
| | Long method | Short method | Without pressure (Hours) | With* (Minutes) |
| Aduki beans | 2-3 | 1 | 1-1½ | 8-10 |
| Black beans | 8-12 | 3 | 1½-2 | 10-15 |
| Black-eyed beans | 8-12 | 2 | 1-1½ | 8-10 |
| Broad beans | 8-12 | 4 | 1½-2 | 10-15 |
| Lima/butter beans | 8-12 | 4 | 1½-2 | 10-15 |
| Chickpeas | 8-12 | 3 | 1½-2 | 10-15 |
| Kidney beans, including Egyptian brown beans (*ful medames*) | 8-12 | 2-3 | 1½-2 | 10-15 |
| Great Northern beans | 8-12 | 2-3 | 1½-2 | 10-15 |
| Haricot beans | 8-12 | 2-3 | 1½-2 | 10-15 |
| Navy beans | 8-12 | 2-3 | 1-1½ | 10-15 |
| Pinto beans | 8-12 | 2-3 | 1-1½ | 10-15 |
| Red kidney beans | 8-12 | 2-3 | 1-1½ | 10-15 |
| Lentils | No soaking needed | | 20-30 minutes (small) 35-40 minutes (large) | 6-10 |
| Mung beans | 8-12 | 45-60 minutes | 45 minutes | 10 |
| Pigeon peas | 8-12 | 2 | 1 | 10 |
| Peas | 8-12 | 2 | 1 | 10 |
| Split peas | No soaking needed | | 20-30 minutes | 6-10 |
| Soya beans | 24 | Do not use this method | 3-4 | 30 |

\* 15 lb pressure cooker.

## Nuts and Seeds

In general, nuts and seeds are delicious and highly nutritious, whether eaten raw on their own or used as part of a recipe. To blanche nuts, put them in a pan of boiling water and allow them to stand for 2-3 minutes (longer for hazelnuts, cobnuts and filberts). Drain, rinse in cold water and rub off the skins.

### Roasting nuts and seeds

Preheat the oven to 325° F (170° C, gas mark 3). Spread the whole or chopped nuts or seeds on a baking tray and place them in the oven. Bake them for about 10 minutes, giving them a shake once or twice during this time. The nuts or seeds are ready when lightly browned.

Nuts and seeds may also be pan-roasted on top of the oven. Put them in an ungreased heavy frying pan and gently toss them over a moderate flame until lightly browned.

## Chicken

Fresh whole chickens or chicken portions tend to taste better than frozen chicken, but for most people the choice is more one of convenience than taste. If you buy a fresh chicken, be sure to choose a reputable retailer. Look for a moist, plump bird with a creamy-coloured skin free from bruising or other discoloration. If the bird is wrapped, check the sell-by date. Store it in the refrigerator on a plate and, if wrapped, break the seal and allow the bird to breathe. Cook it within two days of purchase. Cooked chicken may be safely stored in the refrigerator for three days. Do not freeze fresh chicken unless you are absolutely sure it has not been frozen previously.

You can buy chicken whole and trussed ready for roasting or you can ask the poulterer to cut it into portions for you; alternatively, you can buy several portions of the same cut, such as leg, thigh or breast. The choice depends on what you are cooking and which bit of the bird you enjoy most.

To quarter a chicken yourself, chill it first, as this makes the job easier. Then set it breast side up on a cutting board and, with a long, sharp knife, cut along and through the breast bone. Open the bird out and cut through the back bone, dividing it in two. Cut each half in two by cutting diagonally through the ball and socket joint to give two leg and thigh pieces and two wing and breast pieces. If you wish, it can be further subdivided into ten pieces: two thighs, two drumsticks, two wings, the two breasts each cut into two pieces cross-wise. Use the remaining carcass and giblets for stock.

Chicken has a high protein and a very low saturated-fat content; it also contains some vitamin-B complex. It can thus be a valuable part of a healthy diet. Unfortunately, some producers feed their chickens with hormones and other compounds to accelerate their growth and to change the colour of the flesh. Whenever possible, therefore, buy free-range poultry or at least buy it from suppliers who know how the birds have been reared.

### Types of chicken

*Capon:* a castrated cock, the flesh of which is very tender. The weight of the whole bird should be no more than 4 lb (2 kg).

*Poussin:* a young bird from four to eight weeks old. A poussin should weigh about 1 lb (0.5 kg) and provides one large or two small portions.

*Roasting chicken:* a young tender bird suitable for roasting. A 3-4 lb (1.4-1.8 kg) bird is a convenient weight. Jointed roasting chickens are also good for frying, grilling or for barbecues.

*Boiling fowl:* older, less tender birds used for making soups, stocks and stews.

*Frozen chicken:* these are cleaned and frozen immediately after killing. They are the best type to buy for storage in a home freezer. Once thawed they should not be refrozen.

### Thawing frozen chicken

Prior to cooking, frozen chicken must be thoroughly thawed, preferably in its bag with the seal punctured. Ideally, chicken should be thawed in the refrigerator to ensure that it stays as fresh as possible; in the case of a whole chicken, this means planning ahead.

The following are recommended* thawing times for frozen whole chicken:

| Weight | Thawing at room temperature | Thawing in refrigerator |
|---|---|---|
| 2 lb (1 kg) | 8 hours | 28 hours |
| 3 lb (1.4kg) | 9 hours | 32 hours |
| 4 lb (1.8 kg) | 14 hours | 50 hours |

\* Information provided by British Chicken Information Service.

Always ensure that chicken is thoroughly defrosted before cooking otherwise it will not cook all the way through.

Test to see that there are no ice crystals in the cavity and that the legs and thighs are soft and flexible.

### Cooking methods

*Roasting:* Average cooking times for roast chicken are 20 minutes to the pound plus 20 minutes at 375° F (190° C, gas mark 5).

The use of foil (dull side uppermost) helps to retain the bird's natural juices and reduces the need for basting, but the chicken will require a slightly longer cooking time (for an average 3 lb bird an extra 12-15 minutes). Remove the foil for the last 20 minutes to allow the bird to brown.

To test whether your chicken is cooked, insert a skewer into the thickest part of the thigh. When the juices run out clear, the bird is cooked.

*Microwaving:* Chicken can be both defrosted and cooked in a microwave. However, as models vary, it is most important to check the manufacturer's instructions carefully before proceeding.

*Pressure cooking:* Pressure cooking is a quick and economical method of cooking chicken, but, again, as models vary, you *must* check the instructions of your own particular model. As the cooking time is calculated from the weight of the bird, you must include the weight of the stuffing if stuffing is being used. However, if you are cooking portions of chicken you do not have to increase the cooking time, even if you are cooking eight rather than four portions.

*Slow cooking:* Slow cookers are extremely useful – you can go out all day and come back to a ready-cooked meal. Do make sure the chicken is completely thawed and always cook whole birds on the *high* setting.

*Chicken bricks:* Chicken bricks are a popular way of cooking poultry because the bird will cook in its natural juices, so no added fat is required, and the flavour and nutrients are retained. Soak your chicken brick in water for 15 minutes every time you use it. As soon as you switch on the oven, set the temperature to 275° F (140° C, gas mark 1) and put the chicken brick into the oven for 5 minutes. Then put your chicken into the brick, put it back into the oven and set the dial to the required cooking temperature.

*Roasting bags:* Roasting bags keep the oven clean and brown poultry really well. Flour the inside of the roasting bag before cooking, as this helps the self-basting, and make slits in it before putting it in the oven to prevent the bag from exploding.

# Fish

Fish is expensive compared with chicken, but it is high in protein, a good source of vitamins A and D and low in fat (particularly white fish). What fat there is in fish contains a high proportion of polyunsaturates. Fish is also a versatile food and available in great variety all year round. It is classified into three main groups: white fish (subdivided into round and flat species), where the oil is found in the liver; oily fish, where the oil is dispersed throughout the flesh; and shellfish. The fat content of white fish is usually less than 5 per cent and some varieties like cod and haddock contain less than 1 per cent. Even so-called 'oily' fish contains less fat than many cuts of meat and much of the fat content is polyunsaturated. For instance, the fat content of herring is less than 20 per cent and of this only 20 per cent is saturated fat. Canned fish, which is a handy standby in the pantry, and smoked fish are normally of the oily variety.

## Popular white fish
*Round:* bass, bream, carp, cod, coley, grey mullet, haddock, hake, rock salmon (huss), whiting.

*Flat:* brill, flounder, halibut, plaice, red mullet, skate, sole, turbot.

## Popular oily fish
Eel, herring, mackerel, salmon, salmon trout, sprat, trout, whitebait.

## Popular shellfish
Cockles, crab, lobster, mussels, oyster, prawns, scallops, scampi (Dublin Bay prawns), shrimps.

## Buying fish
Fresh fish must be bought *very* fresh and the best place to go for it is to a reputable fishmonger's. Fresh fish has very little smell, the flesh is firm and elastic, the eyes clear and bright and protruding rather than sunken. The gills should be bright red or pink and not dark-coloured, and the skin should be smooth and shining. Frozen fish should be bought only for convenience. Supermarkets and deep-freezer centres are probably the best places to buy it. Remember when comparing the prices of fish fillets or steaks with

whole fish that a little under a half of a whole fish is often unusable (although the waste can be used for making fish stock), whereas fillets contain no waste. Hence the price difference. The fishmonger will clean out, fillet and skin fish for you or sell you prepared fillets or steaks. If, however, you prefer to do it yourself, it is quite easy and the only equipment you need is a thin, sharp knife (see below).

Shellfish are more susceptible to collecting and concentrating pollutants than other fish and are also more likely to cause stomach upsets if they are not fresh. So it is most important to buy them when they are in season, and fresh from a trusted source, and to use them immediately. Shellfish sold deep-frozen, ready peeled, shelled, dressed and sometimes cooked are normally completely safe to eat, but they are, of course, not as flavoursome as the fresh varieties.

### To clean fish

For both round and flat fish, remove any scales by scraping from tail to head with the dull edge of a knife. Rinse the fish frequently while doing this to wash off the loosened scales. To remove the entrails from a round fish, cut along the abdomen from a point beneath the gills to halfway to the tail. Scoop out the entrails with your fingers and rinse the cavity under running water. Cut off the head and tail if desired. Cut off the fins and gills. For the same operation with a flat fish, cut open the entrail cavity which lies beneath the gills near the head. Remove the entrails as above. Cut off the head and tail if desired. Cut off the fins and gills.

### To fillet a round fish

Clean the fish as above. The head and tail may be left on. Cut the belly from end to end and cut along the entire length of the back of the fish just down to the bone. Turn the knife flat and, working from the belly side and head to tail, cut the flesh away from the bones. Lift the entire side of the fish, in one piece, away from the bones. Turn the fish over and repeat for the other side. If you wish, cut the fillet slantwise into two or three pieces.

### To fillet a flat fish

Clean the fish as above. The head and tail may be left on. Using a sharp, thin knife, cut down the length of the back of the fish following and just reaching the line of the bone. Turn the knife flat and insert it under the flesh on the left-hand side of the fish at the head end, so that the blade is just pressing on the bones. Cut it clear in one piece. Repeat for the right-hand fillet. Now turn the fish over and repeat the operation for the other side of the fish so that you end up with four fillets.

### Cooking methods

Most people are familiar with fish deep fried in batter but fish lends itself to all the basic methods of cooking we generally use in the kitchen. The following resumé of the particular types and cuts of fish most suited to each of the basic cooking methods has been provided by the Fish Industry Authority.

The cooking methods detailed below are suitable for virtually all types of fish, whether whole or filleted, cutlets or steaks. However, there is one golden rule when cooking with fish – never overcook. As fish is naturally tender, it should be cooked for as short a time as possible; prolonged cooking not only toughens the fish, but impairs the flavour, texture and nutritional value. Remember, when cooking with fish, one species of the same type may almost always be substituted for another. For example, when following a recipe for cod, you may use coley or haddock instead.

*Baking:* Most fish may be baked, particularly whole round fish, fillets, cutlets and steaks.

When baking, it is important to retain moisture by using a covered ovenproof dish and by adding liquid such as a little wine, a marinade or melted butter. During the cooking, baste the fish with the liquid to keep it moist and succulent. Alternatively, the fish may be completely enclosed in foil with a knob of butter and herbs.

*Braising or poaching:* Many fish species may be braised or poached and these methods are particularly good for whole fish, thick fillets and large steaks.

The fish is cooked very gently in a liquid, such as milk, wine or the classic fish stock *court bouillon*, sometimes with chopped vegetables, either in the oven or on the hob.

The important thing to remember when cooking fish in small amounts of liquid is that the fish should never be *boiled* in the liquid, as it would overcook and dry out, becoming flaky and unattractive to look at.

*Deep frying:* Many different kinds of fish and shellfish may be deep fried and this method is useful for small whole fish, fillets, thin cuts of large fish and trimmed flat fish.

Deep-fried fish generally needs a protective coating, usually either batter or bread-crumbs. It is most important that the cooking oil reaches the correct temperature before the fish is immersed to ensure that even cooking, a crisp coating and minimum absorption of the cooking oil into the coating are achieved. A standard temperature is 340° F/170° C: at this heat drops of batter sink a little into the hot oil and then quickly float to the surface.

*Grilling:* Grilling is suitable for many whole fish and cuts, and is especially good for small to medium-sized whole fish and fillets.

Whole fish should be scored at the thickest part of the fish to allow the heat to penetrate and cook the fish right through. A little melted butter or oil brushed onto the fish before cooking helps to retain moisture.

*Shallow frying:* Shallow frying can be applied to small whole fish, steaks, cutlets and shellfish.

This is a very quick method of cooking fish in a small quantity of hot oil. Shallow-fried fish is frequently covered in a protective coating of breadcrumbs.

*Steaming:* Steaming is a particularly suitable method for cooking small whole fish, fillets and cutlets.

The fish is cooked in the heat of the steam produced by boiling or simmering liquid. This is an excellent method of cooking fish because it uses no fat and because steamed fish is easily digestible whilst retaining all its nutrients.

To steam a fish or fish fillets without a conventional steamer, very lightly oil a plate large enough to hold the fish, season the fish with lemon juice and salt, and cover it with kitchen foil or another plate. Place the plate over a large pan containing about 2 in (5 cm) of boiling water so that it acts like a lid, and steam the fish until it is tender.

To steam a fish in a regular steamer, very lightly oil a piece of kitchen foil big enough to wrap the fish in. Season the fish and wrap it in the foil. Put the parcel or parcels in the

steamer, put the lid on and steam until the fish is tender (around 10-12 minutes for 8 oz/225 g fillets).

*Microwaving:* Fish cooks well in a microwave oven, retaining its flavour and juices. Microwaves are recommended for baking, braising and poaching fish.

# Eggs, Yoghourt, Cream and Cheese

### Eggs

Eggs contain a lot of high-quality protein. They also contain cholesterol and cholesterol-rich diets have been linked to heart disease. However, in small amounts, cholesterol is an essential nutrient and it is a good idea to include a moderate number of eggs or egg dishes in your diet. Free-range eggs taste better and contain none of the chemicals sometimes present in battery-hen eggs. They cost more but it is worthwhile buying them if you can find a reliable supplier.

### Yoghourt

Yoghourt is an excellent food. It is nourishing, good for the digestion and a versatile ingredient. Yoghourt also has the reputation of promoting longevity and for being a good stamina food. It may be used in the preparation of soups and salads as a marinating agent, in main meals and in desserts, and even as a summer drink mixed with water, a pinch of salt and mint.

Homemade yoghourt is easy to make and is much fresher, tastier and more economical than most of the shop-bought varieties. The process simply involves the addition of live yoghourt to a batch of sterilized plain milk maintained at blood temperature (98° F/37° C). The initial source of live yoghourt can be bought at any health or wholefood store, and after that you just reserve some of your homemade yoghourt to use as the starter for the next batch.

Making yoghourt at home carries some of the mystique attached to breadmaking, but it is basically a simple and foolproof process. Below is a method which should always work. If you do not have the time or inclination to make it, buy live yoghourt from a health or wholefood store. Some of the thick Greek varieties now on sale are excellent in flavour and have a good, firm texture.

### To make yoghourt

Put 1-2 pints (0.5-1 litre) (depending on how much yoghourt you want to make) fresh milk in a clean saucepan and bring to the boil. As soon as it bubbles, switch off the heat and transfer the milk to a clean ceramic or glass bowl. Allow the milk to cook to about blood temperature (98-100° F/37-38° C). To test, put your finger into the milk – it should feel comfortably warm. If you like, you can use a thermometer, although I never do. Now stir in 1-2 tablespoons live yoghourt, cover the bowl with a lid and wrap the whole thing in a thick towel. Store in a warm place (such as the airing cupboard, above the pilot light on a gas stove, above the hot area at the back of the fridge, or in the sun or near a radiator; some people pour the cultured milk into a thermos flask). Leave to set for 10-12 hours, when the yoghourt will be ready for use. Store in the refrigerator for up to a week.

For a thick yoghourt, add 1-2 tablespoons powdered milk to the fresh before starting. If you want to make a really large quantity of yoghourt, make several smaller batches rather than one large one. For some reason it seems to work better that way.

Your first attempt may produce quite a thin, runny yoghourt. Don't worry, this is quite usual. It will get thicker by the third or fourth time of making as your yoghourt culture improves.

Thick yoghourt is a cheap, healthy and simple alternative to whipped cream. It is easily made from your own yoghourt or from shop-bought natural yoghourt. Take a traditional jelly bag and pour in 1 pint (500 ml) of natural yoghourt. Hang the bag over a sink or a large bowl and leave to drain overnight. In the morning gently press the yoghourt and turn it out into a bowl – it is now ready for use. A sieve lined with damp cheesecloth can be used instead of a jelly bag.

### Dairy cream

Dairy creams are delicious but they are rich in saturated fats and should be used only for special treats. The saturated fat content for different types of cream is as follows: double cream, 50 per cent; whipping cream, 40 per cent; sour cream, 28 per cent; single cream, 18 per cent.

Fortunately, there are a number of low-fat dairy products available for use as substitutes for cream in dessert making and for savoury dishes. Traditional standbys are cottage cheese, low-fat curd cheese and thick yoghourt (see above). Three recent imports to British cuisine are detailed below.

*Fromage frais* is as common as yoghourt in France. It is made from fermented skimmed milk, often enriched with a little cream. Fromage frais is smooth-textured and smooth-tasting. It is an excellent alternative to whipped cream although it will not hold a firm shape.

*Crème fraîche* is a traditional accompaniment to fresh fruit desserts. It is a reduced-fat topping rather than a low-fat one. Prepare by gently heating equal quantities of double cream and low-fat yoghourt to a little warmer than blood heat. Pour the cream into a wide-necked vacuum flask and leave overnight. By morning you will have a thick cream. Store in a cool place.

*Coeur à la crème* (so-called because it can be set in little heart-shaped moulds) is a whipped-up cream that looks a lot less healthy for you than it actually is. You need 1 pint (500 g) *fromage frais*, 3 oz (100 g) whipping cream and 2 egg whites. Drain the *fromage frais* (use the same method as for yoghourt above). Lightly whip the cream and fold in the drained *fromage frais*. Whisk the egg whites until they are firm but not dry and fold in the whipped cream, plus 8 oz (225 g) cottage cheese and 8 oz (225 g) low-fat curd cheese.

None of these alternatives to whipped cream will hold a firm shape. If you need a piping cream, beat up a low-fat curd cheese softened with a little Greek yoghourt or similar. Pipe in the usual fashion.

### Cheese

Cheese, apart from being a delicious food and a versatile ingredient for the cook, is also relatively high in protein and a good source of the mineral calcium and vitamins A and D. As with other dairy products, it also contains a fairly high saturated fat content, although traditional cooking cheeses like mozzarella and ricotta contain less than the average

cheese. Cheese should therefore be eaten in moderation in a demivegetarian diet and, where suitable, low-fat varieties should be used for cooking.

*Saturated Fat Contents of Cheeses, Milk and Yoghourt*

|  | % total weight |
|---|---|
| Camembert | 26 |
| Cottage cheese | 4 |
| Cream cheese | 70 |
| Edam | 26 |
| English cheeses (Cheddar, Cheshire, etc.) | 33 |
| Feta | 25 |
| Gouda | 27 |
| Gruyère and Emmenthal | 32 |
| Mozzarella | 19 |
| Parmesan | 26 |
| Ricotta | 15 |
| Milk (whole) | 3.5 |
| Milk (skimmed) | 2 |
| Yoghourt (whole) | 3.4 |
| Yoghourt (low fat) | 1.5 |

### Cooking cheeses

*Cheddar:* a traditional English cheese originally from Somerset. Cheddar-type cheeses are now made all over Britain and are also imported from other countries. Cheddar can be mild or strong in flavour depending on the time it is left to ripen. The texture is smooth and it melts evenly in cooked dishes.

*Cottage cheese:* a low-fat, soft, granular cheese made from skimmed milk. It has a mild flavour and may be used in both savoury and sweet dishes.

*Emmenthal:* a hard Swiss cheese with irregularly spaced large holes. It has a distinctive flavour. Used as for Gruyère.

*Gruyère:* a hard Swiss cheese with regularly shaped small holes. It has a creamy, slightly acid flavour. Melts smoothly for cooking and sauce making. Best known in fondue dishes.

*Mozzarella:* an Italian soft cheese with very little taste of its own, but with excellent melting qualities which make it most useful for the cook, especially in pizza-making. Originally made only from buffalo's milk, the more rubbery cow's milk version is now more common. The best Italian mozzarella is very white, moist and moderately elastic. It is sold for export in plastic bags containing some liquid to keep the cheese fresh. Once opened, store mozzarella in a little lightly salted water in a covered container in the refrigerator.

*Ricotta:* made from cow's or sheep's milk, ricotta is a soft, moist cheese not dissimilar to cottage cheese. It is most useful in savoury dishes with cheese fillings, such as ravioli or filled pancakes, as well as in dessert and cake making. Ricotta is best eaten very fresh and should be bought as needed.

*Parmesan:* a very hard, strong flavoured cheese ideal for grating. Used in cooked dishes and for sprinkling over pasta, soups and polenta.

*Note:* Dishes containing cheese should not be overcooked or overheated. Under such conditions some cheeses, particularly the hard ones, become rubbery, tough and difficult to digest.

# Basic Kitchen Equipment

The recipes in this book do not require any special equipment, although an electric blender is recommended. In fact, in the author's experience, a few essential items of good-quality, hand-operated equipment (except for the blender), together with a sizeable, easy-to-clean work surface and the best cookware you can afford, are the main priorities of good cooking. Below is a list of the suggested basic pieces of kitchen equipment.

### Knives and chopping board

An 8-9 in (20-25 cm) stainless-steel cook's knife, a paring knife and a thin-bladed sharp knife for filleting fish are essentials. Stainless steel is harder to sharpen than carbon steel, but, unlike the latter, it will not blacken or discolour foods such as avocados, red cabbage and fruit. Keep your knives sharp by honing them after use on a steel. For periodic sharpening use an oil stone. Paradoxically, blunt knives are more dangerous than sharp ones since they are more likely to slip. Sharp knives also require less force.

A decent-sized wooden chopping board is a pleasure to work on. Hardwoods such as maple or sycamore are the longest lasting. A wooden board will protect the cutting edge of the knife and provide a good slip-free surface for the food being chopped.

### Blender

This is essential for some recipes and also for those times when you are in a rush. With a blender you can make dressings, dips, sauces, purées and soups in minutes or even seconds. The blender should have its own place on the worktop in a readily accessible position. This is much more convenient and quicker than if it has to be put away in a cupboard after each use.

### Saucepans and a wok

If you can afford them, stainless-steel saucepans are the best. They are hard-wearing, easy to clean and a pleasure to cook with. Enamelware is almost as good, but if it chips the base metal is exposed. Aluminium cookware is to be avoided if possible. It scratches easily and leaves deposits of the metal in the cooking food. It also discolours some vegetables and sauces. Non-stick pans are fine while the coating lasts, but once it starts to wear off they have the same problems as aluminium pans. Perhaps a very good, heavy, non-stick frying pan is a worthwhile buy if it is looked after very carefully. This or a heavy, stainless-steel frying pan may also be used as a substitute for a wok in those recipes where one is recommended.

A wok is the round-bottomed circular pan used in Chinese cooking. It is perfectly designed for stir-fried dishes, deep-frying, sautéing, simmering – in fact, for all the different methods of cooking done on top of the stove. For use on a conventional hot plate or gas ring, a wok needs to be supported on a small metal frame, but this can usually be purchased with the wok.

### Other basic equipment

*Garlic press:* large ones are easier to use and more efficient.

*Lemon or lime juicer:* hand-held, carved wooden ones are the best and simplest.

*Mortar and pestle and/or hand mill:* for grinding spices, nuts and seeds.

*Pepper mill:* black pepper is much better freshly ground.

*Scissors:* useful for preparing vegetables and trimming herbs.

*Vegetable peeler:* swivel-blade ones are the best.

*Kitchen scales:* the simpler the better. Leave set up ready to use on a work top.

*Wooden spoons*

## The Demivegetarian Pantry

Below is a list of basic ingredients which should be kept permanently in stock in your kitchen. Replace them as they are used up.

*Grains and pulses:* long-grain brown and white rice, bulgar wheat, couscous, dried pasta (including egg noodles), red and brown lentils, chickpeas and red beans, your own favourite grains and beans

*Canned goods:* plum tomatoes, chickpeas, red kidney beans, sweetcorn, tomato purée, tinned fish

*Bottled goods:* olives, mustard, chutney

*Nuts and seeds:* sesame seeds, sunflower seeds, walnuts, almonds

*Weekly store:* natural yoghourt, lemons, fresh cream, beancurd, cheese, eggs, fish, chicken

*Dried fruit:* not essential but useful

## Unusual Ingredients

The following ingredients are used in some of the recipes in the book. They should be familiar to the reader, but, just in case they are not, here is a description of each of them and of the ways they are used in cooking.

### Beancurd (tofu)

Beancurd is a soyabean product commonly used throughout the Far East. It is a valuable source of minerals, protein and carbohydrate. Beancurd is now generally available in the West from Chinese grocery stores and health-food shops. It is made from the liquid extracted from crushed soyabeans. Soft in texture, it is usually sold in small square slabs. Covered with water, it will keep for two or three days in the refrigerator. Cut into cubes and added to soups, vegetable or salad dishes, it is delicious. Fried beancurd has a firm yellow crust and can be used in cooked dishes in which fresh beancurd would break up.

### Pressed beancurd

Pressed beancurd may be fried more easily than the tender, fresh, unpressed curd and is less likely to break up in dishes with long cooking times.

To press beancurd, lay the cakes of beancurd on a wooden chopping board. Place a few sheets of kitchen paper on top and then place a plate or flat dish over them. Weight the dish with a cup of water or a scales weight. Finally, tilt the board slightly (rest one end on an upturned saucer) and leave to drain for 1-2 hours. The beancurd will then be pressed and ready to use.

### Beansprouts

Dried beans, particularly soya and mung beans, are sprouted to give tasty white shoots. These beansprouts have become well known and are easily available in the West. Nearly all the beansprouts seen in the shops are grown from mung beans. They are available all the year round and make an excellent fresh, crisp addition to salads, especially in the winter when other vegetables are in short supply. To prepare, simply wash well and drain. Use fresh or stir-fried.

### Bulgar wheat (burghal, bulghar)

A wheat product made since ancient times in the Middle East and other parts of Western Asia: wholewheat grains are parboiled and then dried in the sun. Bulgar has a nutty taste and a fluffy texture. It is very quick and simple to prepare: all that is necessary is to cover it with hot water and leave it for 20-30 minutes.

### Chinese dried black mushrooms

Chinese black mushrooms have a different flavour from the mushrooms we normally use. They are readily available in Chinese grocery stores. They are always sold dried and need soaking for at least 20 minutes in very hot water before use. The stems are tough and inedible and they need to be cut off after the soaking period. See also *Shiitake*.

### Coconut milk

Coconut milk, an ingredient in some Southeast Asian and Indian recipes, is not the liquid inside a coconut, which is called coconut water, but is rather the liquid pressed from grated coconut flesh and diluted with water, or obtained from dried coconut after it has been soaked in hot water or milk, or a mixture of both. Tinned coconut milk is generally available from Chinese or Indian grocery stores. Use the unsweetened variety. Stir it before use. The quality is as good as that of coconut milk made from dried coconut or from the so-called 'fresh' coconuts available in the West.

### Couscous

The national dish of Morocco, Tunisia and Algeria. Couscous is both the name of a grain product made from semolina (itself a wheatgrain product) and the name of a dish which includes couscous as an ingredient. Cooked couscous looks like large white grains of buckshot. It is served in a mountainous heap with a vegetable or sweet sauce poured over the top. To cook, merely cover with hot water and leave for 15 minutes. Then fluff up with a fork.

### Daikon
See *white radish*.

### Fish sauce

Fish sauce is to Southeast Asian cooking what soya sauce is to Chinese or Japanese cuisines. It is made from a liquid extracted from salted fermented shrimps and fish. It is thin in consistency and quite salty. Fish sauce can be bought by that name from Chinese grocery stores.

### Fila pastry

Fila pastry (also called filo or phyllo, or by its Arabic name *ajeen*) is a delicate, paper-thin pastry. It is very versatile and most useful to the pastry cook. The paper-thin sheets of pastry can be used singly or built up into layers of any thickness. They are flexible and can be rolled or folded into a wide variety of shapes. In the Middle East, where fila pastry is very popular, many different pastries in all shapes and sizes and with all kinds of filling are widely available.

Making fila pastry at home requires a lot of skill, patience and time, and nowadays it is normally bought ready prepared. It can be found in good delicatessens and most Greek food stores. Fila pastry is normally sold in standard packs of 1 lb (450 g) or 8 oz (225 g), containing about twenty-four or twelve sheets respectively. The size of a leaf of pastry is usually 50 × 30 cm (20 × 12 in). Commercially produced fila keeps for weeks under refrigeration, but once a pack has been opened or the pastry has been exposed to the heat of the kitchen the sheets start to dry out and become crumbly.

To use fila pastry, remove from the wrapper only as many sheets as you intend to use immediately. Store the unwrapped sheets between two dry tea towels and drape over the top a third tea towel that has been dampened. Remove the individual sheets of pastry from under the tea towels as required and brush them sparsely with melted butter to maintain their flexibility. Do not worry if the sheets tear while you are using them because you can easily repair them with another sheet.

### Miso

Miso is fermented soyabean paste. Naturally fermented miso will keep indefinitely and the flavour improves with age. It is rich in protein and vitamins and forms a basic part of the diet of many countries. It supplies all the essential amino acids and is a good source of vitamin B 12, which is often lacking in a strict vegetarian diet. If carefully fermented, it also contains enzymes which aid the digestion. Miso is traditionally fermented for four or five days, and then aged for two years or more.

35

Miso is a remarkably versatile ingredient. It may be used as a base for soups or sauces, in a marinade for vegetables, as a salad dressing with vinegar or lemon, or added to stock for casseroles or stews.

### Nori

A purple seaweed sold in paper-thin sheets 8 in (20 cm) square, nori is available in Japanese grocery stores in packets of ten sheets. It is used extensively in Japanese cooking for seasoning, garnishing and wrapping other foods. To use nori as a garnish or seasoning, hold a single sheet over a gas flame and wave it about for a few seconds. It will then crumble easily between thumb and forefinger so that you can sprinkle it over the food.

### Shiitake

Shiitake are the Japanese equivalent of Chinese dried black mushrooms. They are tree mushrooms cultivated by injecting fungus into the soft bark of water-soaked tree trunks. They are always sold dried and are reconstituted in the same way as Chinese dried mushrooms. Generally the caps are criss-crossed with light knife cuts before cooking.

### Soya sauce

Soya sauce (*shoyu* in Japanese) is familiar to all Chinese restaurant patrons, although unfortunately the liquid normally found in bottles under this name is a chemically flavoured product which bears little relationship to the real thing. Natural soya sauce is made from a mixture of soyabeans, wheat (or barley) and salt, fermented together for up to two years. The resultant mash is pressed and filtered, and the extracted liquid is heated rapidly to seal in the flavour and stop further fermentation. Make sure when you buy soya sauce you buy one of the fermented varieties. When you use soya sauce be careful not to add too much salt as well since soya sauce is itself salty.

### Tahini

A paste made from crushed sesame seeds, used to make salad dressings and dips.

### White radish

White radish (*daikon* in Japanese, *loh baak* in Chinese) is distinguished by its length, which can be between 6 in (15 cm) and 1 ft (30 cm) or even longer. Despite its looks, it is from the same family as the familiar small red salad radish and it has a definite radish flavour. White radish is excellent raw, sliced or grated, in salads. It also pickles well. It is good in soups and stews and may also be boiled, stir-fried or braised. To prepare, lightly peel and chop or grate as desired.

# SOUPS

Soups are easy to make, nourishing and can be conveniently prepared from a wide variety of ingredients. In the demi-vegetarian diet, vegetables, beans, grains, fish and chicken, individually or in combination, are used for making soups. For instance, a chicken stock may be used as the base of a vegetable soup or leftover chicken may be added to a vegetable stockpot. The recipes given here range from substantial soups which, served with a salad or bread, constitute a filling meal to light soups suited to being served as a starter or as part of a light meal. The recipes are, however, offered only as a guideline: you can, if you wish, substitute or add your own ingredients and flavourings. Remember, the different ingredients in a combination soup are added in accordance with their individual cooking times. Hence chicken and beans first, root vegetables such as potatoes and carrots second, rice and pasta third, and watery vegetables such as spinach and courgettes which cook quickly last. Fish soups are best made with few ingredients and a good stock.

The heart of a fine soup is the quality of the stock, and although stock cubes are convenient and useful on some occasions, the soups you will remember most are those made with homemade stock. In earlier times the stockpot was kept on top of the stove and the cooking water or liquor from vegetables, chicken (or other meat) and beans was added to it. To keep the stock fresh it was boiled every day. Nowadays the best method of ensuring a regular supply of stock for soup and sauce making is to make a large quantity at one time and then to divide it among small plastic containers (say 1 pint/0.5 litre in size) in which it can be deep-frozen and used as needed. Store the cooking water from vegetables, beans or chicken in the refrigerator and add this to your frozen stock when you use it to increase the quantity available. Stock may be made from a wide variety of ingredients but general instructions for basic vegetable, chicken and fish stocks are given below.

Once a stock is made, the range of soups you can prepare is limited only by the ingredients to hand and your imagination.

# Chicken Stock

MAKES 5 PINTS (2.8 LITRES)

*Chicken stock takes some time to make and requires a whole chicken; hence it is worth preparing a decent amount at a time. Use the cooked chicken left over from the recipe in salads, curries, pilavs and other chicken dishes.*

*3-4 lb (1.4-2 kg) medium-quality chicken, quartered*
*7 pints (4 litres) water*
*1 large onion, quartered*
*2 large carrots, chopped*
*2 celery stalks, chopped*
*4-5 bay leaves*
*salt and black pepper to taste*

Put the chicken pieces and water into a large pot and bring to the boil. Skim off any froth that forms and add the other ingredients. Return to the boil, reduce the heat, cover and simmer for 2 hours or more. Strain off the stock. If some of the stock is required immediately, skim off the fat, otherwise let it cool and then refrigerate. Excess solidified fat may then be removed easily.

PREPARATION TIME 2½ HOURS

### Variation

For an oriental-flavoured stock, add 2 teaspoons of grated root ginger to the ingredients and use soya sauce instead of salt.

38

## Vegetable Stock

MAKES 2 PINTS (1 LITRE)

*3 lb (1.5 kg) vegetables (for a stronger-flavoured stock, choose vegetables with a
distinctive flavour such as leeks, onions, parsnips, carrots and celery)
3 pints (1.5 litres) water
2 bay leaves
chopped parsley or other fresh herbs as available
salt and black pepper to taste*

Wash and roughly chop the vegetables and put them into a pan with the other ingredients. Stir well, bring to the boil, reduce the heat, cover and simmer for 45 minutes. Strain off the stock and gently press the vegetables to extract as much liquid as possible. Now discard the vegetables. The stock is ready to use, chill or freeze. If the stock is stored in the refrigerator it should be used within three days.

PREPARATION TIME 1 HOUR

### Variations

1  For a darker-coloured stock, start the recipe by sautéing the onion and other root vegetables in 2 tablespoons (30 ml) vegetable oil until gently browned. Then add the water and other ingredients and proceed as above.
2  For an oriental-flavoured stock, use soya sauce instead of salt and add Chinese or Japanese dried mushrooms to the ingredients.

## Fish Stock

MAKES 3¼ PINTS (1.8 LITRES)

*Fresh fish is quite expensive, but fish stock, which is essential for making good fish
soup, is actually best made from scrap parts of fish, the head, tail and bones, which cost
nothing. The best-tasting stock is made from the scraps of white flat fish such as sole,
halibut and flounder.*

*2 lb (900 g) bones, heads and tails of sole or other fish, washed
1 large leek, chopped
1 large carrot, chopped
½ bunch parsley, chopped
2 sticks celery, chopped
juice of 1 lemon
4 pints (2.2 litres) water
salt and black pepper to taste*

Put all the ingredients into a large pan and bring slowly to the boil. Reduce the heat and simmer, covered, for 1 hour. Occasionally remove the lid and skim off any scum that has formed. Strain off the stock. Use immediately or refrigerate or deep-freeze. If refrigerated, use within two to three days.

PREPARATION TIME 1 HOUR 15 MINUTES

▼▼▼▼▼▼▼▼▼▼▼▼▼▼▼▼▼▼▼▼▼▼▼▼▼▼▼▼▼▼▼▼▼▼▼▼▼▼

## Mouth-Popping Chicken Soup
### SERVES 6

*This is a substantial soup which can be served on its own as a light meal or with rice for
a more filling meal. It is a very flavoursome soup and a favourite with people who like
spicy food.*

2 lb (1 kg) chicken pieces
2 pints (1 litre) water
2 tablespoons (30 ml) vegetable oil
1 medium onion, diced
2 cloves garlic, crushed
1 tablespoon (15 ml) crunchy peanut butter
1-2 teaspoons curry powder
½ teaspoon chilli powder
½ teaspoon ground ginger
3 oz (75 g) Chinese noodles covered in hot water for 5 minutes, rinsed in cold water
and drained
salt to taste
juice of 1 lemon

Put the chicken pieces into a heavy saucepan, cover with 2 pints (1 litre) of water, bring
to the boil, reduce the heat, cover, and simmer for 45 minutes or until the chicken is
tender.

Meanwhile put the oil in a frying pan and lightly fry the onion and garlic. Stir in the
peanut butter, curry powder, chilli powder and ginger, and lightly cook for 2 minutes,
then remove from the heat. Remove the cooked chicken from the stock and cut the meat
and skin away from the bones. Skim off any fat that has settled on top of the stock and
then leave the stock to simmer. Chop the meat and skin into small pieces and add them to
the frying pan. Coat the meat in the spice mixture and transfer the contents of the frying
pan to the stock. Bring to the boil, add the noodles, adjust the seasoning, add the lemon
juice, stir well and serve.

Cooked rice may be used instead of noodles.

PREPARATION TIME 1 HOUR

▼▼▼▼▼▼▼▼▼▼▼▼▼▼▼▼▼▼▼▼▼▼▼▼▼▼▼▼▼▼▼▼▼▼▼▼▼▼

## Chicken, Lemon and Coconut Milk Soup
### SERVES 4

*This is a Southeast Asian soup. It is spicy, hot, creamy and filling. With rice or bread,
it serves as a light meal. Tinned coconut milk is readily available in stores selling
Indian or Chinese groceries. Ordinary milk may be used instead.*

*¾ pint (450 ml) water*
*¾ pint (450 ml) coconut milk*
*2 chicken breasts or legs, skinned, boned and chopped into bite-sized pieces*
*2 teaspoons grated lemon rind*
*2 spring onions, finely chopped*
*½-1 fresh or dried red chillies, seeded and finely sliced*
*juice of 1 lemon*
*2 tablespoons (30 ml) fish or soya sauce*
*crushed roasted peanuts to garnish (optional)*

Put the water and coconut into a heavy-bottomed saucepan and bring them slowly to the boil. Add the chicken pieces and lemon rind and simmer, uncovered, for 20 minutes or until the chicken is tender. Add the spring onions and chillies, and simmer for a further 2-3 minutes. Stir in the lemon juice and fish or soya sauce, garnish with roasted peanuts, and serve immediately.

*Note:* Coconut milk curdles if it is heated too quickly or boiled too fast. Cook the soup uncovered so that you can be sure it simmers gently.

PREPARATION TIME 30 MINUTES

## *Mushroom and Barley Miso Soup*
### SERVES 4

*This is not only a lovely soup but one that is good for people recovering from an illness or an upset stomach. It is nutritious, easy to digest and the miso will help settle the system.*

*3 tablespoons (45 ml) vegetable oil*
*1 large onion, chopped*
*2 teaspoons chopped fresh thyme or 1 teaspoon dried thyme*
*12 oz (350 g) mushrooms, chopped*
*1 tablespoon (15 ml) pot barley, washed*
*2 pints (1.1 litres) water or stock*
*1 teaspoon miso*
*1 small clove garlic, crushed*
*salt to taste*
*finely chopped fresh parsley to garnish*

Heat the oil in a saucepan or pressure cooker and sauté the onions and thyme. After 5 minutes add the mushrooms and cook for a further 2 minutes. Add the pot barley and the water or stock. Bring to the boil, reduce the heat, cover and cook for 1-1½ hours (or 30 minutes under pressure). Liquidize ¼ pint (150 ml) of the soup in a blender with the miso, garlic and salt. Pour the blended soup back into the saucepan, mix well, reheat and serve with lots of chopped parsley to garnish.

PREPARATION TIME 1½ HOURS (INCLUDING 1 HOUR SIMMERING)

## Turkish Onion Soup

### SERVES 4–6

*Onion soup is popular in Iran and Turkey as well as in France. Its preparation is
similar to French onion soup, but the seasoning is different. The soup may be served
with croutons and grated cheese; alternatively, lightly beaten eggs can be whipped into it
just before serving.*

2 fl oz (50 ml) olive oil
1 lb (450 g) onions, thinly sliced
1 oz (25 g) wholemeal flour
2½ pints (1.4 litres) water
salt and black pepper
½ teaspoon turmeric
1 teaspoon sugar
juice of 1 lemon
2 teaspoons dried mint
½ teaspoon ground cinnamon
2 eggs, lightly beaten, or 4-6 slices of French bread and 4 oz (100 g) Parmesan cheese

Heat the oil in a heavy pan and add the onions. Cook for 15 minutes over gentle heat,
stirring occasionally. Use a little of the water to make a paste with the flour and stir this
into the onions. Stirring constantly, continue to cook the onion and flour mixture for 2 to 3
minutes. Add the rest of the water and bring to the boil. Reduce the heat and season to
taste with salt and black pepper. Add the turmeric, sugar and lemon juice, cover and
leave to simmer for 45 minutes or longer. Adjust the seasoning. Rub the mint to a
powder, mix with the cinnamon and stir the mixture into the soup. Remove from the
heat. Now stir the lightly beaten eggs into the soup and serve.

Alternatively, leave out the eggs and lightly toast the slices of French bread. Put one
piece in each bowl, pour the soup over them, and serve with Parmesan cheese.

PREPARATION TIME 1 HOUR (INCLUDING 45 MINUTES SIMMERING)

## Lettuce and Hazelnut Soup

### SERVES 4

*During the summer months, when life seems like one long lettuce, this soup is
impressive enough for a grand occasion. It is also refreshing served chilled.*

1 large lettuce
½ medium onion
1 oz (25 g) butter
¾ pint (350 ml) light chicken stock, heated
sea salt and freshly ground black pepper
2 tablespoons (30 ml) single cream
1½ oz (40 g) chopped hazelnuts

Wash the lettuce and then blanch it in a pan of boiling, lightly salted water. Drain it well, reserving the water. Chop the onion and cook slowly in the butter until transparent. Add the lettuce roughly chopped and cook for about 3-4 minutes. Then add the heated stock. (If using a stock cube, dissolve it in the lettuce water.) Simmer, covered, for 20 minutes. Liquidize the cooked vegetables until very smooth and then season to taste with salt and black pepper. Serve garnished with cream and chopped hazelnuts.

PREPARATION TIME 30 MINUTES

# Carrot and Coriander Soup

SERVES 4–6

*Fresh green coriander is now available all year round from Indian grocery stores and good greengrocers. It gives this soup a distinctive and excellent flavour. Carrots make a light, slightly sweet soup. Other root vegetables such as parsnips or potatoes may be used instead of, or as well as, carrots.*

*2 teapoons vegetable oil*
*1 medium onion, finely chopped*
*1 lb (450 g) carrots, peeled (or just scrubbed if young carrots)*
*and finely chopped*
*1½ pints (900 ml) stock or 1½ pints (900 ml)*
*water and milk in equal quantities*
*2 tablespoons (30 ml) finely chopped fresh coriander*
*salt and black pepper to taste*
*yoghourt or single cream to garnish*
*freshly ground coriander seeds to garnish*

Heat the oil in a heavy-based saucepan and sauté the onions and carrots until softened but not browned. Add the stock or water and milk and bring to the boil. Reduce the heat, cover and simmer for 20 minutes. Stir in the coriander leaves. Ladle threequarters of the soup into a liquidizer and gently pulse the machine until the soup is smooth. Return it to the pan, season with salt and black pepper and heat through. Serve in a tureen or individual bowls garnished with a small swirl of yoghourt or cream and a pinch of ground coriander.

PREPARATION TIME 30 MINUTES

*Variation*
For a creamier soup, replace the stock or milk and water mixture with all milk, skimmed or unskimmed.

▼▼▼▼▼▼ ▼▼▼▼▼▼ ▼▼▼▼▼▼ ▼▼▼▼▼▼ ▼▼▼▼▼▼ ▼▼▼▼▼▼ ▼▼▼▼▼▼ ▼▼

# Black-Eyed Pea Soup with Croutons
## SERVES 4

*This is a simple but very tasty soup, and with the addition of croutons it makes a hearty
beginning to a meal.*

*1 tablespoon (15 ml) vegetable oil*
*3 cloves garlic, crushed*
*8 oz (225 g) black-eyed peas, soaked overnight and drained*
*1½ pints (900 ml) water or stock*
*1 tablespoon (15 ml) chopped fresh parsley*
*1 tablespoon (15 ml) chopped fresh mint*
*salt and black pepper to taste*

Put the oil into a heavy saucepan, add the garlic and sauté over a moderate heat until
golden. Add the black-eyed peas and water or stock and bring to the boil. Cover, reduce
the heat, and simmer until the peas are tender (about 45 minutes). Five minutes before
the end of the cooking time, stir in the parsley and mint and season with salt and black
pepper. The thickness of the soup can be adjusted with water or stock as required. Serve
with the croutons in a separate bowl.

### Croutons
To make croutons you need good, firm bread. A single ⅜ in (1 cm) slice from a 2 lb
(1 kg) loaf will make enough croutons for three to four persons.

Take a 5 in (12 cm) pan, and add vegetable oil to a depth of ⅜ in (1 cm) and place over
a medium heat. Meanwhile remove the crusts from the bread and cut the slices into ⅜ in
(1 cm) cubes. When the oil has just begun to haze, test its temperature by dropping in
one of the bread cubes. It should turn quite rapidly to a golden-brown colour. Rescue the
cube from the oil, reduce the heat slightly and drop in enough of the bread cubes to cover
loosely the bottom of the pan. When these cubes are nicely browned, lift them out with a
slotted spoon and drain them on absorbent kitchen paper. Repeat the process until all the
bread cubes are used. Croutons are best eaten fresh but will keep for a day or two in an
airtight container.

### Grilled croutons
Take a French loaf and cut it into ⅜ in (1 cm) slices. Spread both sides of each slice with
butter or brush them liberally with olive oil. Lightly toast both sides of the bread under
the grill. Serve them as they are or spread one side with thyme-flavoured goat's cheese
or a mixture of equal quantities of Stilton and soft Camembert or pounded anchovies or
anything that takes your fancy. Toast lightly and serve.

PREPARATION TIME 1 HOUR
SOAKING TIME 12-24 HOURS

## Fresh Tomato Soup

SERVES 4

*Make this soup in the summer months when tomatoes are good, cheap and plentiful and fresh basil and oregano are easily available.*

*2 tablespoons (30 ml) olive oil*
*1 medium onion, finely chopped*
*2 cloves garlic, crushed*
*2 lb (900 g) ripe tomatoes, chopped*
*1 tablespoon (15 ml) tomato purée*
*1 tablespoons (15 ml) chopped fresh basil or 1 teaspoon dried basil*
*½ tablespoon (7.5 ml) chopped fresh oregano or ½ teaspoon dried oregano*
*salt and freshly ground black pepper*
*1 pint (550 ml) vegetable stock*

Heat the olive oil in a heavy saucepan and sauté the onion and garlic, stirring, until lightly browned. Add the tomatoes, tomato pureé, herbs and salt and black pepper to taste. Stir over a moderate heat until the tomatoes are broken up. Stir in the stock and bring to the boil. Reduce the heat, cover, and simmer for 30 minutes. Towards the end of the cooking period adjust the seasoning to taste.

PREPARATION TIME 45 MINUTES

## Leek and White Wine Soup

SERVES 4–6

*Most leek and potato-based soups are of a smooth consistency. This one is different. It has a chunky texture. It also, unusually, contains a fair amount of wine.*

*4 large or 8 small leeks*
*2 oz (50 g) butter*
*4 medium potatoes, peeled and diced*
*1 pint (550 ml) chicken stock*
*½ pint (275 ml) dry white wine*
*sea salt and freshly ground black pepper*
*2 tablespoons (30 ml) chopped fresh parsley*

Wash the leeks and cut the white parts crosswise into thin slices. Sauté them gently in the butter. Add the potatoes to the pan and sauté for a few minutes. Add the stock and wine and bring to the boil. Simmer until the potatoes are tender and just starting to fall apart. Season to taste with the salt and black pepper. Add the parsley just before serving. Serve very hot.

PREPARATION TIME 30 MINUTES

## Chilled Apple and Apricot Soup
SERVES 6

*1 medium onion, peeled and chopped*
*1 tablespoon (15 ml) sunflower seed oil*
*1 tablespoon (15 ml) mild curry powder*
*12 oz (350 g) cooking apples, peeled, cored and chopped*
*8 oz (225 g) dried apricots, chopped*
*14 oz (400 g) tinned tomatoes*
*1½ pints (800 ml) chicken stock*
*1 teaspoon lemon juice*
*salt and freshly ground black pepper*
*honey to taste (optional)*
*4 fl oz (100 ml) natural yoghourt*
*1 tablespoon (15 ml) flaked almonds, dry-roasted*

Sauté the onion very gently in the sunflower seed oil until soft and transparent. Stir in the curry powder. Add the apples, apricots, tomatoes and chicken stock. Bring to the boil, add the lemon juice, salt and black pepper. Lower the heat and simmer for 30 minutes. Taste and add a little honey if too sharp. Liquidize the mixture and recheck the seasoning. Allow to cool and then chill thoroughly in the fridge.

   To serve; stir the yoghourt vigorously to obtain a smooth consistency and thin down if necessary with a little water so that it falls attractively when poured into the soup. Scatter the toasted flaked almonds on top.

PREPARATION TIME 25 MINUTES
CHILLING TIME 4 HOURS

## Bamboo Shoots and Green Bean Soup
SERVES 4–6

*This Indonesian soup is served with boiled rice. Some of the soup stock is used to moisten the rice, the vegetables are then spooned over it and the stock is served in a separate bowl. Vegetables other than green beans can be used. See variations below.*

*2 pints (1.1 litres) vegetable stock*
*1 medium onion, finely diced*
*2 cloves garlic, crushed*
*1 in (2.5 cm) root ginger, finely chopped*
*1 lb (450 g) tomatoes*
*2 bay leaves or daun salem leaves*
*salt and pepper*
*1 lb (450 g) green beans, topped, tailed and cut into 2 in (5 cm) lengths*
*4 oz (100 g) tinned bamboo shoots, sliced*
*1 tablespoon (15 ml) lemon juice or tamarind water*

Heat the stock in a pan and add the onion, garlic and ginger. Bring to the boil, cover and set to simmer. Scald the tomatoes briefly in boiling water, remove the skin and chop them into quarters. Put the tomatoes into the stock pan, add the bay leaves or daun salem leaves, stir well and season to taste with salt and pepper. Leave the soup to simmer for another 15 minutes. Add the green beans and bamboo shoots, stir well and return the pan to the boil. Reduce the heat to low and simmer, covered, for 15-20 minutes or until the beans are very tender. Stir in the lemon juice or tamarind water, adjust the seasoning and serve with boiled rice.

PREPARATION TIME 45 MINUTES

### Variations

1 For the green beans you can substitute carrots, potatoes, courgettes, aubergines or cabbage.
2 Replace the bamboo shoots with sliced water chestnuts.

# Rich Vegetable and Rice Soup

SERVES 4–6

*This is a flavoursome sweet-sour soup which is filling and nutritious.*

2 tablespoons (30 ml) vegetable oil
1 large onion, chopped
1 teaspoon dried basil
1 bay leaf
1 tablespoon (15 ml) wholemeal flour
1 small carrot, scrubbed and chopped
1 stick celery, chopped
1 teaspoon honey or brown sugar
1 tablespoon (15 ml) cider vinegar
14 oz (400 g) canned tomatoes, chopped (reserve juice)
1 pint (550 ml) water
1 small clove garlic, crushed
soya sauce and/or salt to taste
2 fl oz (50 ml) milk
4 oz (100 g) cooked rice
2 tablespoons (30 ml) roasted sunflower seeds to garnish

Heat the oil in a pan and sauté the onion, basil and bay leaf for 5 minutes. Stir in the flour. Add the carrot, celery, honey or sugar, cider vinegar, tomatoes with their juice and the water. Bring to the boil, reduce the heat, cover and cook for 20 minutes. Liquidize the soup in a blender with the garlic, soya sauce and/or salt. Add the milk and cooked rice. Reheat and serve with a sprinkling of roasted sunflower seeds.

PREPARATION TIME 45 MINUTES

# Lemon Garlic Fish Soup

### SERVES 6

*This is an all-purpose fish soup which can be made with any white fish. The method includes the preparation of a fish stock, but if you have some already available you can use it and ignore the first part of the recipe.*

*2 lb (1 kg) white fish, filleted (reserve skin, head and bones)*
*2½ pints (1.5 litres) water*
*1 lb (450 g) tomatoes*
*1 teaspoon grated lemon rind or freshly chopped lemon grass*
*1 medium onion, diced*
*2 cloves garlic*
*1 teaspoon grated root ginger*
*1 tablespoon (15 ml) lemon juice or tamarind water*
*salt and pepper*

Put the reserved skin, bones and head of the filleted fish (but not the fish) into a pan with the water. Bring to the boil, reduce the heat, cover and simmer for 1 hour. Drain off and reserve the stock and discard the bones. Scald the tomatoes briefly in boiling water, skin and chop them. Put the stock back into the pan, add the tomatoes and lemon rind or lemon grass and bring to the boil. Reduce the heat and leave to simmer. Put the onion, garlic, ginger and 1 tablespoon (15 ml) of the fish stock into a blender or food processor and blend them to a paste. Alternatively, dice the onion and garlic very small and with the ginger crush them in a pestle and mortar to a paste. Add the paste to the stock, stir well and simmer for 5 minutes. Cut the filleted fish into pieces, add to the stock and simmer for 20 minutes. Stir in the lemon juice or tamarind water, season to taste and serve.

PREPARATION TIME 1½ HOURS
(OR 30 MINUTES IF FISH STOCK IS AVAILABLE)

*Top: Mouth-Popping Chicken Soup in ladle (page 40) Right: Lettuce and Hazelnut Soup (page 42)*
*with Goat's Cheese Croutons (page 44) Left: Black-Eyed Pea Soup (page 44)*

*Top right: Thai Prawn Salad (page 52) Bottom right: Cucumber and Feta Cheese (page 58)*
*Bottom left: Olives Marinated with Lemon and Coriander (page 57) Top left: Pitta Bread*

# STARTERS

The starters for this chapter have been chosen to illustrate the variety of different styles of dishes that may be used as the first course of a meal. They could also be served in combination with one another to provide interesting and colourful meals or as part of a buffet. This is very much the way *mezze*, Middle Eastern hors d'oeuvres, are served, and I have devoted part of the chapter to *mezze* dishes. Remember when planning a menu that, according to demivegetarian ideas, if you serve a fish- or chicken-based starter, the main course should be essentially vegetarian.

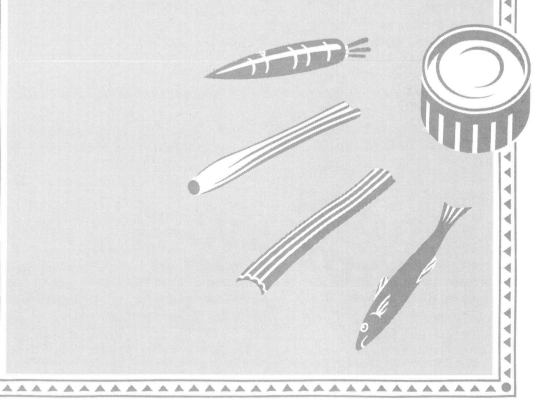

▼▼▼▼▼▼▼▼▼▼▼▼▼▼▼▼▼▼▼▼▼▼▼▼▼▼▼▼▼▼▼▼▼▼▼▼▼

# Aubergine and Coriander Pâté
### SERVES 4–6

*This pâté illustrates that a vegetable pâté can be just as delicious as a meat or a fish one.
Pine nuts, which develop a distinctive and likeable flavour when toasted, are used in
the recipe. However, they are expensive and if you wish you could substitute other nuts
such as walnuts or hazelnuts.*

*2 medium-sized aubergines*
*2 cloves garlic*
*2 oz (50 g) pine nuts or hazelnuts or walnuts, dry-roasted*
*2 tablespoons (30 ml) olive oil*
*1 tablespoon (15 ml) lemon juice*
*salt and black pepper*
*2 tablespoons (30 ml) finely chopped coriander leaves*
*sprigs of coriander to garnish*

Preheat the oven to 400° F (200° C, gas mark 8). Wrap the aubergines in foil and bake in
the oven for 30 minutes or until soft. Skin and roughly chop them and put them into a
blender or food processor. Add the garlic, nuts, oil, lemon juice and salt and pepper to
taste and purée. Taste and adjust the seasoning if necessary. Stir the coriander leaves
into the pâté and divide it between four to six ramekins. Refrigerate until needed.
Garnish each ramekin with a sprig of coriander to serve.

### PREPARATION TIME 40 MINUTES

▼▼▼▼▼▼▼▼▼▼▼▼▼▼▼▼▼▼▼▼▼▼▼▼▼▼▼▼▼▼▼▼▼▼▼▼▼

# Kipper Pâté
### SERVES 4–6

*This is a quick-to-make, low-fat but tasty smoked-fish pâté. Serve with thin toast as a
starter or with a salad and bread for a light meal.*

*12 oz (350 g) kipper fillets, skinned*
*6 oz (175 g) low-fat cottage or curd cheese*
*2 tablespoons (30 ml) natural yoghourt or* fromage frais *(see p.00)*
*1 teaspoon lemon juice*
*black pepper to taste*
*finely chopped parsley or dill to garnish.*

Place all the ingredients except the parsley or dill in a food processor or blender and
purée. Divide the pâté between four to six ramekin dishes. Refrigerate, covered, until
required. Garnish each ramekin with finely chopped parsley or dill to serve.

### PREPARATION TIME 15 MINUTES

# Watermelon and Prawn Creole

SERVES 6

*This is an old favourite which Jules looks forward to making every summer when watermelons are in season. It is full of contrasting tastes and textures.*

*1 small onion, chopped*
*1 small eating apple, peeled and chopped*
*1 oz (25 g) butter*
*2 teaspoons honey*
*1 tablespoon (15 ml) mild curry powder*
*2 tablespoons (30 ml) dry white wine*
*2 teaspoons grated fresh ginger*
*salt and freshly ground black pepper*
*1 tablespoon (15 ml) apricot jam*
*2 teaspoons tomato purée*
*4 fl oz (100 ml) whipping cream*
*4 tablespoons (60 ml) thick mayonnaise*
*1 small watermelon*
*1 small green pepper*
*4 oz (100 g) large shelled prawns*

Sauté the onion and apple in the butter in a small saucepan for a few minutes. Add the honey, curry powder, wine, fresh ginger and salt and black pepper, and simmer gently in a covered pan until the apple and onion are very soft. Add a little water if the mixture gets too dry. Leave to cool. Then rub the mixture through a sieve with the apricot jam. Stir in the tomato purée.

Whip the cream until just thick. Fold it with the mayonnaise into the apple mixture and chill thoroughly.

Just before serving, scoop out the watermelon flesh in small neat pieces, preferably with a melon baller, extracting the black seeds as you go. Set aside six pieces of melon and six prawns to garnish. Cut the pepper into thin strips about 1 inch (2.5 cm) long.

To assemble, combine the melon pieces, prawns and pepper strips and add enough of the curried cream to coat them well. Arrange in individual dishes and decorate with the reserved prawns and watermelon.

PREPARATION TIME 45 MINUTES
CHILLING TIME 2 HOURS

## Variation

Any surplus curried dressing is delicious with cooked chicken.

# Thai Prawn Salad with Dressing
### SERVES 4

*This is a simple starter. It looks delicious served on sparkling white plates.*

## Salad
*8 oz (225 g) cooked peeled prawns*
*2 in (5 cm) cucumber, seeded and finely sliced*
*1 medium green pepper, seeded and finely sliced*
*1 medium tomato, diced*
*1 small onion or ½ Spanish onion, finely sliced*

## Dressing
*1 tablespoon (15 ml) cider or rice wine vinegar*
*2 tablespoons (30 ml) fish sauce or soya sauce*
*3 tablespoons (45 ml) lemon juice*
*¼ teaspoon chilli sauce*
*¼ teaspoon white sugar*

## Garnish
*2 spring onions, finely sliced*

Place all the salad ingredients in a serving bowl. Combine the dressing ingredients and mix well. Pour the dressing over the salad and toss. Chill for 30 minutes or longer. When you are ready to serve the salad, drain it well and divide it between four small white plates. Garnish with spring onion rings.

### PREPARATION TIME 15 MINUTES
### CHILLING TIME 30 MINUTES

# Gingered Crab
### SERVES 4

*This Japanese starter is especially delicious with fresh crab, but tinned crabmeat is a good alternative.*

*½ cucumber*
*salt*
*2 teaspoons sugar*
*2 fl oz (50 ml) cider vinegar*
*2 teaspoons soya sauce*
*6 oz (175 g) fresh crabmeat (from 2-3 crabs) or tinned crabmeat*
*1 tablespoon (15 ml) grated fresh root ginger*
*2 spring onions, finely chopped*

Cut the cucumber in half and scoop out the seeds with a teaspoon. Slice the flesh across into thin half-moon shapes. Soak the slices in salted water (2 tablespoons/30 ml salt to 2 pints/1 litre water) for 20 minutes, then transfer them to iced water to keep fresh. Combine the sugar, cider vinegar, soya sauce with 2 fl oz (50 ml) water in a small pan and bring very slowly to the boil. Remove from the heat and leave to cool to room temperature. Shred the crabmeat finely and set it aside in the refrigerator to chill. Drain the cucumber slices and gently press out as much water as possible between sheets of absorbent paper. Using a garlic press, squeeze the juice from the grated ginger. Add juice to the vinegar dressing to taste. Combine the crabmeat and cucumber slices in a serving bowl. Sprinkle them with the vinegar and ginger dressing and mix well. Garnish with spring onions and serve.

PREPARATION TIME 30 MINUTES

# Fried Aubergine or Courgette Slices
### SERVES 4

*I have given two recipes here, one for a chilled aubergine dish and the other for a hot courgette dish, but the aubergines and courgettes may be interchanged.*

*2 small aubergines, cut into ⅜ in (1 cm) thick slices*
*4 fl oz (100 ml) olive oil*
*2 cloves garlic, thinly sliced*
*2 tablespoons (30 ml) cider vinegar*
*salt*

Put the aubergine slices in a colander and generously salt them. Set aside for 30 minutes. Now wash and drain them and pat them dry. Fry the slices in the oil in a heavy frying pan until they are soft and browned on both sides. Lay the slices in a shallow dish, sprinkling each layer with garlic slices, vinegar and salt to taste. Chill and serve.

*4 small courgettes, sliced lengthwise*
*2 tablespoons (30 ml) vegetable oil (olive oil if possible)*
*2 cloves garlic*
*salt to taste*
*2 tablespoons (30 ml) cider vinegar*

To make this Turkish dish, put the courgette slices in a colander and salt them generously. Set aside for 30 minutes. Now wash and rinse them and pat them dry. Heat the oil in a heavy frying pan, add the garlic and sauté lightly. Add the courgette slices and brown them on both sides. Place them in a serving dish, season with salt and sprinkle the vinegar over them. Serve hot.

PREPARATION TIME 45 MINUTES
CHILLING TIME WHERE APPLICABLE 1 HOUR

# Spinach and Cream Cheese Spring Roll with Fila Pastry

### SERVES 4

*Frozen fila pastry (see p.35) is becoming increasingly easier to find in good delicatessens and supermarkets, and nowadays this recipe is convenient to prepare.*

*1 lb (450 g) fresh spinach*
*½ medium onion, finely chopped*
*sunflower seed oil for shallow frying*
*4 sheets of fila pastry (the remainder of the packet should be quickly wrapped in polythene and stored in the fridge)*
*4 oz (100 g) cream cheese*
*1 nutmeg*
*salt and freshly ground black pepper*

Wash the spinach very well and cook gently without further water in a covered, heavy-duty saucepan. When completely wilted, drain into a colander and leave for 15 minutes weighted with a small plate so that all the excess water drains away. Meanwhile sauté the chopped onion in a little sunflower seed oil until soft and transparent. Then chop the spinach roughly on a board.

Lay out the four sheets of pastry on a tea towel. Brush the upper surface of the first sheet with oil and fold in half. Brush the upper surface of the now folded pastry and fold in half across. Put a quarter of the spinach, onion and cream cheese in neat layers at one end of the folded pastry and season with grated nutmeg, salt and pepper. Then roll up the pastry to make a parcel measuring about 3½ × 1½ in (9 × 4 cm), turning in the sides after the first roll to make tidy edges. Repeat with the remaining three sheets. Shallow fry the parcels in more sunflower seed oil, turning frequently until the pastry is golden brown. Drain on absorbent paper and serve hot with a simple salad garnish.

### PREPARATION TIME 45 MINUTES

## Variation
Cooked chicken or smoked salmon (omit the salt) can be used in addition to the ingredients listed above.

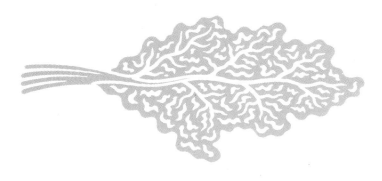

## Pear and Avocado Salad with Tahini Mayonnaise
SERVES 4

*This very elegant-looking starter is quick to prepare. The sauce is quite addictive and larger quantities can be made up and stored for a week or so in the fridge to accompany other dishes such as cold salmon or chicken, or as a dip for raw vegetables.*

*2 teaspoons tahini paste*
*1 tablespoon (15 ml) mayonnaise*
*2 tablespoons (30 ml) natural yoghourt*
*1 medium-sized ripe avocado*
*1 ripe pear*
*2 limes*
*chicory to garnish*

Combine the tahini, mayonnaise and yoghourt and mix well together. Peel the avocado and the pear and divide them into halves or quarters lengthways, removing the stone and core. Cut the fruit into fairly thin slices lengthwise. Divide the slices between four plates, making a fan shape of alternate slices. At the base of the fan, place 1 tablespoon (15 ml) of the tahini mayonnaise. Slice one of the limes and arrange as a garnish with the chicory leaves. Squeeze the juice of the second lime over the pear and avocado fans.

PREPARATION TIME 15 MINUTES

## Traditional French Crudités
TO SERVE – VARIOUS

*Not a single salad but a collection of the very simplest salads mixed with the simplest dressings. Try some of the following to accompany a light meal of cold chicken, smoked fish, hard-boiled eggs, sardines and the like:*

*raw carrots scrubbed clean, finely grated and dressed with lemon juice*
*raw shelled broad beans sprinkled with coarse sea salt*
*lightly cooked beetroot the skins rubbed off, cubed and mixed with a small amount of creamed horseradish sauce*
*cucumber, peeled, cut into finest rounds, dressed with good white wine or cider vinegar and left to marinate for 30 minutes*
*capsicums, seeded, cut into thin circles and steeped in olive oil*
*firm tomatoes, sliced, lightly dressed with vinaigrette and sprinkled with freshly ground black pepper and chopped parsley*

PREPARATION TIME ABOUT 30 MINUTES FOR 4 PEOPLE

## Various Mezze

*Mezze or Middle Eastern hors d'oeuvres are an intrinsic part of the culture of the*
*Middle Eastern world. They are served, like the Western hors d'oeuvres, at the*
*beginning of a meal as appetizers or alternatively in greater variety as a meal in itself.*
*Mezze also make excellent snacks and accompaniments to drinks. Below I give a list of*
*simple mezze ideas. All the items may be prepared quickly and a selection of them will*
*provide an unusual and exciting start to a meal. In the following recipes are other more*
*substantial ideas for mezze dishes. Serve mezze with warmed pitta bread.*

*olives, on their own or in salad dressings or spiced with a little cayenne*
*nuts, a single variety or mixed, plain or roasted*
*slices of onion and tomato arranged in a circle of alternating rings, garnished*
*with chopped parsley or mint*
*wedges of cucumber*
*yoghourt, slightly salted*
*chickpeas, soaked, drained, roasted in the oven and salted*
*pickles*
*French beans, cooked and dressed in oil and lemon juice*
*tinned artichoke hearts or okra, drained and dressed in olive oil*
*slices of salted or smoked fish*
*cottage cheese or yoghourt or both, mixed with tahini and spinkled with cumin*
*seeds*
*raw vegetables, shredded, chopped or sliced*
*slices of hard-boiled egg, dusted with cinnamon, coriander and salt*
*lemon wedges*
*radishes on ice*
*fried prawns*
*fresh dates stuffed with soft cheese*
*fresh dates in yoghourt*
*tahini seasoned with crushed garlic and lemon juice to taste*
*ripe avocado flesh mixed with finely chopped onion and tomato, seasoned with*
*salt and black pepper, dressed with lemon juice and served on lettuce leaves*

## Individual Mezze Dishes

*The following recipes may be used as part of a selection of mezze or individually as*
*conventional starters.*

## Olives Marinated with Lemon and Coriander

*Ideally the olives should be marinated for at least a week for the full flavour of the lemon and coriander to be absorbed. Thus this part of a mezze needs advance planning. The recipe uses 2 lb (900 g) olives. You will not need that many at any one time, but the olives will keep for a long time and will be delicious at a later date.*

*2 lb (900 g) black or green olives (drain off any brine)*
*2 tablespoons (30 ml) coriander seeds*
*2 small lemons, thinly sliced*
*olive oil*
*sprigs of parsley to garnish*

Pick over the olives and discard any bruised ones. With a thin, sharp knife cut two or three shallow slits into each. Wash them well under running cold water and drain. Prepare two clean 1 lb (450 g) pickling jars. Put the olives into a bowl and combine them with the coriander seeds. Pack the mixture into the jars, adding slices of lemon evenly throughout each jar as you proceed. Pour olive oil slowly into each jar until it reaches the brim. Seal the jars and store in a cool place for at least a week before serving. Serve garnished with sprigs of parsley.

PREPARATION TIME 15 MINUTES MARINATING TIME 1 WEEK

## Chicken Meatballs

SERVES 4

*This recipe is very good for using up leftover cooked chicken. The meatballs can be served as a main dish with a yoghourt or tomato sauce.*

*1 thick slice white or brown bread*
*1 lb (450 g) cooked chicken, minced*
*1 egg, beaten*
*½ teaspoon cumin powder*
*¼ teaspoon cayenne (optional)*
*pinch of saffron or turmeric*
*salt and black pepper*
*2 tablespoons (30 ml) finely chopped parsley*
*vegetable oil for frying*
*lemon wedges to garnish*

Cut the crusts off the bread and dip the bread into a bowl of water. Remove it and squeeze out as much water as possible. Put the bread, chicken, egg, spices, salt and black pepper to taste and parsley into a bowl and knead them into a homogeneous mixture. Form the mixture into walnut-size balls and fry them nicely brown in shallow oil. Serve them with lemon wedges and squeeze lemon juice over them before eating.

PREPARATION TIME 30 MINUTES

▼ ▼ ▼ ▼ ▼ ▼ ▼ ▼ ▼ ▼ ▼ ▼ ▼ ▼ ▼ ▼ ▼ ▼ ▼ ▼ ▼ ▼ ▼ ▼ ▼ ▼ ▼ ▼ ▼ ▼ ▼ ▼

## Cucumbers with Feta Cheese
### SERVES 4

*If feta cheese is not available, crumbly Lancashire or a similar cheese can be
substituted.*

*1 medium cucumber, peeled and diced*
*1 medium onion, finely diced*
*6 oz (175 g) feta cheese*
*2 tablespoons (30 ml) olive oil*
*juice of 1 lemon*
*salt and black pepper*

Combine the cucumber and onion and mix well. Crumble the feta cheese into a separate
bowl, and beat in the oil, lemon juice, and salt and black pepper to taste. Pour the mixture
over the cucumber and onion and serve.

PREPARATION TIME 20 MINUTES

▼ ▼ ▼ ▼ ▼ ▼ ▼ ▼ ▼ ▼ ▼ ▼ ▼ ▼ ▼ ▼ ▼ ▼ ▼ ▼ ▼ ▼ ▼ ▼ ▼ ▼ ▼ ▼ ▼ ▼ ▼ ▼

## Prawn Pâté
### SERVES 4

*This pâté which, except for the prawns, requires no cooking, is, as far as I know, of
Egyptian origin.*

*1 lb (450 g) fresh prawns, shelled, or 8 oz (225 g) tinned prawns*
*4 oz (100 g) coarse breadcrumbs*
*1 oz (25 g) butter*
*6 black or green olives, stoned and chopped*
*2 oz (50 g) nuts (almonds, pine or walnuts), lightly roasted*
*juice of 1 lemon*
*2 tablespoons (30 ml) finely chopped parsley*
*2 cloves garlic, crushed*
*½ teaspoon ground ginger*
*½ teaspoon cumin*
*salt and black pepper to taste*

Fry the fresh prawns in a little oil until tender. If using tinned prawns omit this stage.
Combine all the ingredients, except for four prawns, in a liquidizer and blend the mixture
until smooth. Transfer the pâté to four ramekin dishes and top each with a whole prawn.
Serve with slices of lemon, olives and pitta bread.

PREPARATION TIME 20 MINUTES

# SALADS AND DRESSINGS

Salads should be colourful, delicious, economical and nutritious. The colour and taste are achieved by careful choice of ingredients and dressing, the economy by buying salad vegetables in season, and the nutrition by eating raw foods. Many studies published in recent years have confirmed the importance of raw foods in our diets, because, unlike cooked foods, none of their original nutrients, fibre and the enzymes essential to good digestion are destroyed by cooking.

Recipes for particular salad combinations that work well together are given here, but creating your own salads is also fun. To do this successfully there are certain basic rules to follow, just as in any other branch of the culinary arts. Paddy Byrne, one of my restaurant partners, wrote the following guidelines for salad making for a book we collaborated on called *Seasonal Salads* (now out of print in this country). The advice he gives is excellent and with his permission it is reprinted here.

At the end of the chapter is a selection of recipes for standard and unusual dressings.

## General Guidelines for Salad Making

1  Use only the very best and freshest ingredients.

2  Be selective about what goes into a salad since a thoughtless collection of vegetables will appeal neither to the tongue nor the eye. A great many salads are spoilt by the introduction of extra ingredients. Add nothing without considering how it will affect the final taste and appearance of the salad.

3  Do not roughly chop up all salad ingredients similarly. Respect the characteristic shape of each vegetable and how it is seen to its best advantage. This may mean cutting cabbage into long corrugated strips, peppers into their sectional rings, cutting beef tomatoes horizontally to show off their wonderful map of the world cross-section, and leaving thin twig-like French beans uncut. If you have several salads to prepare, see that you cut each in a different manner. Indeed, if you are presenting a large buffet, prepare some salads by hand and some by machine to give even greater visual variety.

4  Remember that strong-tasting vegetables such as garlic or onions used in small quantities as flavourings will need chopping up very finely in order to distribute that flavouring evenly. Large, bland, starchy vegetables must also be cut or sliced small to enable the dressing to penetrate easily.

5  Beware unhappy combinations: for example, tomato and beetroot or radish and radichio, whose colours clash horribly, or celery and fennel, which look alike and crunch in a similar manner and give an effect on the taste buds reminiscent of tasting coffee when you thought you were about to taste tea. Beans, lentils and other starchy foods are usually best served as separate salads as they muddy the clean taste of many more delicate ingredients.

6  Many of the joys of salads are found in their crisp textures and sharp colours. Thus it is essential that no salad vegetables are overcooked and that any green vegetables, once cooked, are quickly chilled under running or iced water to arrest the cooking process and preserve the texture and colour.

7  Season and mix salads adequately, although in the light of recent findings it may be wise to use salt with discretion. Those who salt their cooked meals well will obviously not enjoy unsalted salads. Cabbage, dried beans, lentils and, of course, potatoes all need more salt than most vegetables. Pulses need plenty of vinaigrette to give an edge to their earthy taste.

8  Match dressings and solid ingredients carefully. For instance, light, subtle dressings will be lost on coarse flavoured pulses or strong-flavoured endive, but strong-flavoured dressings would swamp the taste of, say, delicate lettuce or fresh immature broad beans.

9  Don't add too many different fresh herbs to your salads. All you are likely to do is to overload and confuse the palate.

## Winter Salad Bowl

### SERVES 4

*A colourful and nutritious salad of lightly cooked winter vegetables. The vegetables given here are only suggestions and you could use other combinations that suit your taste according to availability. Serve on its own or with sliced cold chicken.*

60

*4 oz (100 g) cauliflower florets*
*4 oz (100 g) green beans, topped, tailed and cut diagonally into 2 in (5 cm)*
*lengths*
*4 oz (100 g) carrots, peeled, cut in half and then into sticks*
*4 oz (100 g) fresh or frozen peas*
*1 small head of lettuce*
*4 oz (100 g) cooked beetroot, sliced*
*1 tablespoon (15 ml) lemon juice*
*3 tablespoons (45 ml) olive oil (or other vegetable oil)*
*salt and freshly ground black pepper to taste*

Bring a small pan of salted water to the boil and individually parboil the cauliflower, green beans, carrots and peas for 5-10 minutes or until each is just *al dente* or crunchy. The process can be speeded up by using more than one pan of boiling water. Drain the vegetables and allow them to cool. Shred the lettuce into a serving bowl. Place the cauliflower florets in the centre of the bed of lettuce and arrange the green beans, carrots, peas and beetroot around them in separate groups. Combine the lemon juice, oil, salt and black pepper and mix well. Carefully dribble a little of the dressing over each of the clumps of vegetables, leaving about 1 tablespoon (15 ml) dressing in reserve. Chill the salad for 30 minutes and then sprinkle it with the remaining dressing and serve.

PREPARATION TIME 40 MINUTES
CHILLING TIME 30 MINUTES

*Variation*
For a more substantial salad, sprinkle grated cheese over the top.

## Spinach and Apple Salad with Lime Dressing
SERVES 4

*In the West Indian autumn and winter months, limes are sometimes as cheap as lemons, and lime juice is a worthy alternative to lemon juice as a salad dressing. In this salad the sharpness of the lime juice sets off the sweetness of the apple and the flavour also enhances the harsh taste of the spinach.*

*1 lb (450 g) fresh spinach*
*2 tablespoons (30 ml) vegetable oil*
*1 tablespoon (15 ml) lime juice*
*2 medium eating apples, chilled, cored, quartered and chopped into small pieces*
*salt and black pepper to taste*

Cut the thick stalks off the spinach and discard. Wash, drain and finely shred the leaves. Combine the oil and lime juice and whisk well together. Mix the spinach and the apple and add the dressing. Season with salt and black pepper and toss the salad.

PREPARATION TIME 15 MINUTES

## Marinated Aubergine Salad
### SERVES 4–6

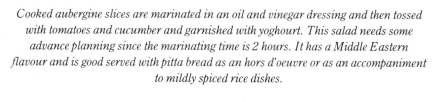

*Cooked aubergine slices are marinated in an oil and vinegar dressing and then tossed with tomatoes and cucumber and garnished with yoghourt. This salad needs some advance planning since the marinating time is 2 hours. It has a Middle Eastern flavour and is good served with pitta bread as an hors d'oeuvre or as an accompaniment to mildly spiced rice dishes.*

*2 small aubergines, sliced*
*3 fl oz (75 ml) olive oil*
*2 fl oz (50 ml) wine vinegar*
*2 cloves garlic, crushed*
*1 tablespoon (15 ml) lemon juice*
*1 teaspoon dried basil*
*salt and black pepper to taste*
*½ cucumber, thickly sliced*
*2 medium tomatoes, quartered*
*2 tablespoons (30 ml) natural yoghourt*

Lightly brush the aubergine slices on both sides with some of the oil and grill them under a moderate grill until just browned and tender enough to push a fork through easily. Cut the aubergine slices into quarters. Combine the remaining oil, vinegar, garlic, lemon juice, basil, salt and black pepper in a bowl and mix well. Add the aubergines while they are still warm. Transfer the bowl to a refrigerator and leave for about 2 hours. Stir in the cucumber and tomatoes, top with a dollop of yoghourt and serve.

PREPARATION TIME 20 MINUTES
CHILLING TIME 2 HOURS

## Fennel, Tuna and Walnut Salad
### SERVES 4

*A simple but very tasty salad.*

*1 medium-sized bulb fennel, finely chopped*
*8 oz (225 g) tinned tuna fish, drained and shredded*
*4 oz (100 g) walnuts, chopped*
*4 oz (100 g) mushrooms, sliced*
*1 tablespoon (15 ml) vegetable oil*
*salt to taste*

Combine the fennel, tuna and walnuts in a serving bowl. Lightly sauté the mushrooms in the oil. Stir the mushrooms and oil into the bowl and season with salt.

PREPARATION TIME 10 MINUTES

# Lentil, Tomato and Anchovy Salad

SERVES 4–6

*Lentil salads are colourful, filling and versatile. Try using different salad ingredients
from those suggested in the recipe. The anchovies in the salad give it a good flavour.
Serve it as a main-dish salad.*

8 oz (225 g) whole green or brown lentils
½ medium onion, chopped
1 clove garlic, crushed
1 bay leaf
4 tablespoons (60 ml) olive oil
1 tablespoon (15 ml) wine vinegar
1 tablespoon (15 ml) lemon juice
½ teaspoon French mustard
salt and black pepper to taste
1 small green pepper, seeded and chopped
4 tomatoes, skinned and chopped
2 sticks of celery, sliced
2 oz (50 g) tinned anchovy fillets, drained and chopped
2 tablespoons (30 ml) chopped parsley
black olives to garnish

Put the lentils, onion, garlic and bay leaf in a pot, barely cover with water and simmer, covered, until the lentils are just tender (45-60 minutes). Drain, transfer to a serving bowl and set aside to cool. Combine the olive oil, vinegar, lemon juice, mustard, salt and black pepper and whisk well together. Stir this dressing into the lentils while they are still warm so that it is absorbed. Leave to cool to room temperature. When cool, stir the green pepper, tomatoes, celery, anchovies and parsley into the lentils and adjust the seasoning if necessary. Garnish with a few black olives and serve.

PREPARATION TIME 1 HOUR 15 MINUTES (INCLUDING 45 MINUTES
TO COOK THE LENTILS)

## Variation

If you are in no hurry for the salad, its flavour improves if it is chilled and marinated for 1-2 hours.

## Coriander and Beancurd with Sesame Sauce
### SERVES 6

*In this Chinese recipe coriander leaves are used as a main ingredient rather than just as a flavouring. Combined with beancurd, peanuts and a sesame sauce, they give a strong-flavoured and unusual dish which, served cold, makes an excellent salad.*

*12 oz (350 g) fried beancurd (see p.155)*
*8 oz (225 g) peanut oil*
*4 oz (100 g) unsalted peanuts*
*12 oz (350 g) fresh coriander leaves, trimmed and washed*

*Sesame sauce*
*3 tablespoons (45 ml) light soya sauce*
*3 tablespoons (45 ml) sesame oil*
*2 teapoons sugar*
*salt to taste*

Drain the fried beancurd on absorbent kitchen paper and allow to cool. When cool, slice as thickly and as uniformly as possible. Put aside in a bowl.

Heat the peanut oil and, when almost smoking hot, turn off and add the peanuts. Cook, stirring with a wooden spoon, 30-40 seconds, until the peanuts are golden brown. Drain and reserve the oil for another time. Spread the nuts on paper towels to remove the excess oil.

Drop the coriander leaves into 1½ pints (900 ml) boiling water, then drain immediately. Chill under cold running water and squeeze by hand to remove excess moisture.

Chop the leaves finely and add them to the beancurd. Toss to blend. Spoon the mixture onto a serving dish and scatter the peanuts over the top. Blend the ingredients for the sauce and pour it over the coriander and beancurd mixture. Serve cold.

PREPARATION TIME 25 MINUTES

## Minted Spinach and Yoghourt Salad
### SERVES 4–6

*A flavoursome salad which may be prepared all year around. Serve it as a side dish or with hot bread as a starter.*

*10 oz (275 g) fresh spinach, trimmed and washed*
*1 small onion, chopped*
*1 clove garlic, crushed*
*1 tablespoon (15 ml) olive oil*
*6 fl oz (175 ml) natural yoghourt*
*salt and black pepper*
*2 teaspoons chopped fresh mint or ½ teaspoon dried mint*
*2 oz (50 g) walnuts, chopped*

*Top: French Bean and Black Olive Salad (page 67) Bottom: Fiery Fish Salad (page 71)*

*Left: Stir-Fried Vegetables with Tofu (page 79) Right: Stuffed Aubergine Vegan Style (page 84)*

Cook the spinach leaves in a heavy pan until tender without extra water. Drain and chop it coarsely. Gently brown the onion and garlic in the olive oil and set aside to cool. Stir the yoghourt into the spinach, add the onion and garlic and season to taste with salt and black pepper. Arrange the salad on a serving plate and sprinkle the mint and walnuts over the top. If using dried mint, crush it between your fingertips as you sprinkle it. Chill for 15 minutes before serving.

PREPARATION TIME 20 MINUTES
CHILLING TIME 15 MINUTES

*Variation*
Frozen spinach, defrosted and cooked, may be substituted for fresh spinach.

# *Banana, Bamboo Shoot and Tomato Salad*

SERVES 4

*A traditional Chinese food, bamboo shoots are versatile and convenient, adding crunch and variety to an otherwise ordinary salad. Keep a tin in the cupboard. Here bamboo shoots are combined with two everyday ingredients to produce an unusual and delicious salad.*

*1 banana, peeled and sliced*
*juice of 1 lemon*
*4 medium tomatoes, sliced*
*4 oz (100 g) tinned bamboo shoots, drained and sliced*
*3 tablespoons (45 ml) vegetable oil*
*¼ teaspoon curry powder*
*salt to taste*
*freshly ground black pepper to garnish*

Sprinkle the banana slices with a little of the lemon juice. In a large salad bowl or in individual dishes, carefully arrange the banana, tomato and bamboo shoot slices in colourful layers. Whisk together the remaining lemon juice, oil, curry powder and salt and pour this dressing over the salad. Top with a little freshly ground black pepper to serve.

PREPARATION TIME 15 MINUTES

*Variation*
This salad also works well with a yoghourt dressing (see over).

## Cheese Salad with Lime and Yoghourt Dressing
### SERVES 4

*An unusual but very good salad. Serve it with olives, a green salad and crusty French bread. If limes are unavailable, use lemon juice.*

*8 oz (225 g) Cheddar or Gruyère or Emmenthal cheese cut into ½ in (1 cm) cubes*
*1 large green pepper, seeded and chopped*
*2 medium tomatoes, quartered*

*Yoghourt dressing*
*4 fl oz (100 ml) natural yoghourt*
*juice of 1 lime*
*½ teaspoon (2.5 ml) French mustard*
*small pinch cayenne*
*½ teaspoon (2.5 ml) dried basil*

Combine the cheese cubes with the pepper and tomatoes. Beat together the yoghourt, lime juice, mustard, cayenne and basil. Stir this mixture into the cheese salad. Chill and serve.

## Solange's Green Salad
### SERVES 4

*Solange was once the French consul in Liverpool. She was a wonderful cook and being invited to her house for dinner was a treat to be looked forward to. This very simple but delicious green salad recipe was given to me by her.*

*1 teaspoon lemon juice*
*1 teaspoon wine vinegar*
*4 teaspoons sunflower seed oil*
*1 tablespoon (15 ml) finely chopped fresh chervil or 1 teaspoon dried chervil*
*salt and black pepper*
*2 oz (50 g) chopped walnuts*
*1 crisp lettuce, separated into leaves, washed and drained*

In a salad bowl whisk together the lemon juice, wine vinegar, sunflower seed oil, chervil, and salt and black pepper to taste. Add the walnuts; then, just before serving, add the lettuce and toss it in the dressing. As Solange said, 'If they meet too early the lettuce loses all its crispness and freshness.'

PREPARATION TIME 10 MINUTES

# Russian Winter Salad

SERVES 6

*A substantial hot mustard salad dressed in sour cream and designed to keep the
Siberian cold at bay.*

6 oz (175 g) cooked beetroot, peeled and diced
6 oz (175 g) cooked but firm potatoes, peeled and diced
2 medium eating apples, cored and diced
2 medium carrots, peeled and diced
1 tablespoon (15 ml) prepared mustard
4 tablespoons (60 ml) vegetable oil
salt
4 tablespoons (60 ml) sour cream

Combine the beetroot, potatoes, apples and carrots. Stir the mustard into the oil to form
a paste. Stir this into the beetroot mixture, season with salt to taste and set aside for 1
hour. Just before serving, stir in the sour cream.

PREPARATION TIME 20 MINUTES (INCLUDING COOKING POTATOES)

# French Bean and Black Olive Salad

SERVES 4

*Young French beans at their best should be crisp and snap easily when broken in two.
They need only a minimum of cooking and, when cooked, should still have some
crunch. Two variations on this salad which make it more substantial are given below.*

1 lb (450 g) young French beans, topped only
salt
2 oz (50 g) black olives
4 tablespoons (60 ml) olive oil
2 tablespoons (30 ml) lemon juice
black pepper

Put the beans in a large pan of salted boiling water and cook for 10 minutes or less. Drain
them, rinse immediately under cold running water, drain again and then put them into a
salad bowl. Stone and chop four or five of the olives and leave the rest whole. Add the
whole olives to the beans with the oil, lemon juice and black pepper. Toss well and chill
slightly. Serve garnished with the chopped olives.

PREPARATION TIME 20 MINUTES

## Variations
1 Add two or three quartered hard-boiled eggs before serving.
2 For an unusual and nutritious variation, add 6 oz (175 g) beancurd, pressed (see p. 34)
and then fried in a little oil.

# Fennel and Grapefruit Salad

SERVES 4 .

*It is often the simplest combinations that work best and so it is with this salad. The sharp, juicy grapefruit seems to be the perfect partner for the crunchy, aniseed-flavoured fennel.*

*1 lb (450 g) bulb fennel, washed and trimmed*
*2 grapefruit, peeled and the pith removed*
*2 tablespoons (30 ml) olive oil*
*½ teaspoons salt*
*fennel leaf sprouts to garnish*

Cut and throw away the hard cores of the fennel bulbs. Slice the bulbs into thin sections and place these in a mixing bowl. Cut the grapefruit into slices and pull these apart over the mixing bowl, letting the chunks fall over the fennel. Discard any skin or other indigestible matter which is easily removed. Add the olive oil and the salt and mix thoroughly. Garnish with the fennel leaves and serve.

PREPARATION TIME 20 MINUTES

# Salade Niçoise

SERVES 4 AS A SIDE DISH

*Salade Niçoise is well known but still worth inclusion in a demivegetarian recipe book. In Salade Niçoise raw and lightly cooked vegetables are combined with a little cooked fish and olives, and dressed in an olive oil and lemon juice dressing. The oil is polyunsaturated and the combination of ingredients is well balanced between protein, vitamins, minerals, fibre and carbohydrates. The salad is also delicious.*

*1 small crisp lettuce, shredded*
*1 lb (450 g) tomatoes, quartered*
*8 oz (225 g) French beans, lightly cooked in a little water*
*1 small bunch watercress*
*1 green pepper, seeded, cored and sliced*
*8 oz (225 g) cooked or tinned tuna fish, drained and flaked*
*2 oz (50 g) mixed green and black olives, stoned.*

### Dressing
*2 fl oz (50 ml) olive oil*
*3 tablespoons (45 ml) fresh lemon juice*
*salt and black pepper to taste*

Arrange the ingredients nicely in a salad bowl. Mix the dressing, pour it over the salad and distribute gently. Chill before serving.

PREPARATION TIME 15 MINUTES

## Brown Rice and Bean Salad

SERVES 4–6

*Rice and beans are complementary protein partners, and weight for weight this salad has the same amount of usable protein as a piece of steak. Do not, however, think it will be heavy and boring. The finished salad looks moist, colourful and tempting, and tastes good. If red beans are not available, use chickpeas or haricot beans.*

*8 oz (225 g) cooked or tinned red beans, drained (equals 4 oz/100 g raw beans)*
*10 oz (275 g) cooked brown rice, rinsed and cooled*
*(equals 5 oz/150 g raw brown rice)*
*3 tablespoons (45 ml) mayonnaise (see p. 72)*
*3 tablespoons (45 ml) cider vinegar*
*2 cloves garlic, crushed*
*1 tablespoon (15 ml) lemon juice*
*2 tablespoons (30 ml) finely chopped parsley*
*salt and black pepper to taste*
*1 medium carrot, peeled, cut into matchsticks*
*1 green pepper, seeded and diced*
*1 stick celery, finely chopped*

Combine the beans, rice, mayonnaise, vinegar, garlic, lemon juice, parsley, salt and black pepper and gently mix well together. Set the mixture aside in the refrigerator to chill for 30 minutes and to give the beans and rice time to absorb the dressing. Now lightly mix in the carrot, pepper and celery, and serve.

PREPARATION TIME 1 HOUR (INCLUDING COOKING THE RICE)
SOAKING TIME 12 HOURS (OR USE TINNED BEANS)

## Red Cabbage in Juniper Cream and Yoghourt Sauce

SERVES 6

*A colourful salad which goes particularly well with cold chicken.*

*1 lb (450 g) red cabbage*
*3 fl oz (75 ml) whipping cream*
*12 juniper berries, ground or finely crushed*
*2 teaspoons cider or wine vinegar*
*salt to taste*

Remove the outer leaves of the cabbage and the bitter core. Now shred it finely (if you are using a knife use a stainless steel one). Combine the cabbage with the other ingredients, mix them well together and serve.

PREPARATION TIME 15 MINUTES

# Aioli with Crudités

SERVES 4–6

*In this recipe plain, crisp raw vegetables are served with aioli sauce. Refreshing and simple.*

*8 sticks of celery, cut in half*
*6 medium carrots, cut into sticks*
*1 medium cucumber, cut into 3 in (7.5 cm) lengths and quartered*
*2 green peppers, sliced*
*small bunch of radishes, trimmed*

## Aioli
*6-8 garlic cloves*
*1 medium egg yolk, beaten*
*salt*
*9 fl oz (250 ml) olive oil*
*white pepper*
*juice of 2 medium lemons*

Prepare the vegetables and arrange them decoratively in a serving bowl. Cover with clingfilm and chill in the refrigerator for about 1 hour. Put the garlic, egg yolk and a little salt in the blender and, with the machine running, add the oil very slowly to form a thick sauce. Season with salt, pepper and lemon juice. Pour the sauce into a large serving bowl or three or four small ones, cover with clingfilm and leave in the refrigerator until needed. Serve the aioli and vegetables together and allow the diners to help themselves.

PREPARATION TIME 30 MINUTES
CHILLING TIME 1 HOUR

### Variation
Grate the vegetables coarsely (in this case you might substitute beetroot for radishes) and then arrange them in little piles on individual plates. Place a large spoonful of aioli on each plate.

## Beancurd Dip with Crudités

*Follow the recipe above but replace the aioli with a low-fat beancurd dip.*

*Beancurd dip*
*4 oz (100 g) beancurd, drained*
*2 cloves garlic*
*4 shallots*
*¼ teaspoon ground ginger*
*2 tablespoons (30 ml) chopped fresh parsley or coriander or other fresh herbs*
*salt and pepper to taste*

Combine all the ingredients in a liquidizer and blend until smooth.

## Fiery Fish Salad
### SERVES 4

*This Thai fish salad is very hot, so if you prefer a mild salad reduce the quantity of chillies. Serve with chilled cucumber slices which cool and refresh the mouth between mouthfuls of salad.*

*2 × 8 oz (225 g) white fish fillets*
*1 tablespoon (15 ml) vegetable oil*
*2 shallots or 1 small onion, finely sliced*
*2 teaspoons grated root ginger*
*2 oz (50 g) roasted peanuts, coarsely crushed*
*2 tablespoons (30 ml) lemon or lime juice*
*1 teaspoon grated lemon or lime rind*
*½ red chilli, seeded and finely chopped*
*½ green chilli, seeded and finely chopped*
*½ teaspoon salt*
*½ crisp lettuce, leaves washed and drained*
*coriander leaves, finely chopped, to garnish*

Fry the fish in the oil until lightly browned on both sides and cooked. Set aside to cool. Combine all the remaining ingredients except the lettuce and garnish and mix well. Flake the fish into a mixing bowl and stir in the chilli dressing. Make a bed of lettuce in a serving dish, pile the fish salad in the middle, garnish with coriander leaves and serve.

PREPARATION TIME 30 MINUTES

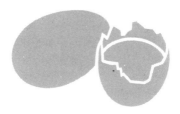

# Dressings
## Basic Mayonnaise
MAKES ABOUT 10 FL OZ (300 ML)

*1 large egg*
*1 teaspoon prepared mustard*
*good pinch salt*
*9 fl oz (250 ml) vegetable oil*
*wine vinegar (up to 2 tablespoons/30 ml) to taste*
*additional salt and black pepper to taste*

Break the egg into a bowl or liquidizer and add the mustard and salt. Beat or blend at medium speed until the mixture thickens slightly. Still beating, pour in the oil from a measuring jug, drop by drop initially and then, as it begins to thicken, in a slow but steady stream until all the oil is absorbed. Carefully beat or blend in the lemon juice or wine vinegar and season to taste with the salt and black pepper. Store in a cool place. Mayonnaise will not keep for much longer than a day.

PREPARATION TIME 5 MINUTES

### Variations
The following are some of the possible ways of giving mayonnaise a different flavour. The amounts given are approximate. They are suitable for use with ¼ pint (150 ml) mayonnaise.

*Caper:* 2 teaspoons chopped capers
     1 teaspoon chopped pimento
     ½ teaspoon tarragon vinegar

*Celery:* 1 tablespoon (15 ml) finely chopped celery
     1 tablespoon (15 ml) finely chopped chives

*Cucumber:* 2 tablespoons (30 ml) chopped cucumber
     ½ teaspoon salt

*Herbs:* 2 tablespoons (30 ml) chopped fresh chives
     1 tablespoon (15 ml) chopped fresh parsley

*Lemon:* Add the finely grated rind of 1 lemon and use lemon juice (same amount) instead of vinegar in the preparation of the mayonnaise.

*Spinach:* 3 spinach leaves, lightly blanched and finely chopped
     1 tablespoon (15 ml) finely chopped parsley
     2 tablespoons (30 ml) finely chopped chives

## Basic Vinaigrette Dressing

MAKES 6 FL OZ (175 ML)

*5 fl oz (120 ml) vegetable oil*
*2 tablespoons (30 ml) wine vinegar, cider vinegar or lemon juice*
*salt and pepper to taste*
*1 teaspoon prepared mustard (optional)*

Place all the ingredients in a bowl or liquidizer and beat or blend well. Test and adjust seasoning if necessary.

PREPARATION TIME 5 MINUTES

## Green Vinaigrette Dressing

MAKES 5 FL OZ (150 ML)

*This dressing goes well with starch-rich vegetables such as courgettes or sweet vegetables like tomatoes or beetroot with pasta.*

*5 fl oz (120 ml) olive oil*
*2 tablespoons (30 ml) lemon juice*
*2 oz (50 g) parsley, larger stems removed*
*1 teaspoon prepared mustard*
*salt and pepper to taste*

Place all the ingredients in a liquidizer and blend first at medium speed and then at high speed until they form a smooth emulsion. Test for seasoning and adjust if necessary.

PREPARATION TIME 5 MINUTES

## Coconut Dressing

MAKES 8 FL OZ (225 ML)

*This Southeast Asian dressing goes well on cooked and uncooked vegetable salads.*

*4 oz (100 g) fresh coconut, grated, or 4 oz (100 g) desiccated coconut moistened with 2 tablespoons (30 ml) hot water*
*½ small onion, finely diced*
*pinch chilli powder or ¼ teaspoon hot pepper sauce*
*2 tablespoons (30 ml) lemon juice*

Put all the ingredients into a blender and briefly pulse the machine to form a homogeneous but not completely smooth mixture.

PREPARATION TIME 5 MINUTES

# Green Garlic Dressing
MAKES 5 FL OZ (150 ML)

*This dressing goes well with starch-rich vegetables such as courgettes or sweet vegetables such as tomatoes or beetroot, or with pasta. Don't be tempted to be mean with the parsley. The sharp green colour is half the pleasure of the dressing.*

*2 cloves garlic*
*4½ fl oz (120 ml) olive oil*
*2 tablespoons (30 ml) lemon juice*
*2 oz (50 g) parsley, larger stems removed*
*1 teaspoon prepared mustard*
*salt and pepper to taste*

Place all the ingredients in a liquidizer and blend first at medium speed and then at high speed until a smooth emulsion is achieved. Test the seasoning and adjust if necessary.

PREPARATION TIME 10 MINUTES

*Variation*
Add 2-3 oz (50-75 g) tinned tuna fish to the ingredients.

# Japanese Mustard Dressing
MAKES 4–5 TABLESPOONS (60–75 ML)

*Use instead of vinaigrette dressing or with individual lightly cooked vegetables.*

*1 teaspoon prepared English mustard*
*2 tablespoons (30 ml) rice vinegar or cider vinegar*
*1 tablespoon (15 ml)* shoyu *(natural soya sauce)*
*1-2 teaspoons sugar*

Combine the mustard, vinegar and *shoyu* in a small mixing bowl, add sugar to taste and stir well until it dissolves.

PREPARATION TIME 5 MINUTES

# Tahini Dressing
MAKES 16 FL OZ (450 ML)

*The most popular Middle Eastern dressing, tahini dressing can be poured over almost any fresh or cooked vegetable or served as a dip with hot bread. It is very simple and quick to make. If necessary the sauce can be thinned down with water or more yoghourt. Tahini paste is produced by finely grinding sesame seeds. It is widely available in ethnic food stores and wholefood shops.*

*5 fl oz (150 ml) tahini paste*
*5 fl oz (150 ml) natural yoghourt*
*4 fl oz (100 ml) lemon juice*
*1-2 cloves garlic, crushed*
*3 tablespoons (45 ml) finely chopped parsley*
*½ teaspoon ground cumin or ¼ teaspoon cayenne pepper*
*salt to taste*

Combine all the ingredients in a mixing bowl and beat together. Taste for seasoning. Unused dressing will keep for two or three days in the refrigerator.

PREPARATION TIME 5 MINUTES

# Beancurd Dressing
SERVES 4–6

*Fresh white beancurd has the remarkable ability to carry a whole gamut of flavours. Blend it with a little liquid, add your flavouring, be it mustard, paprika, honey, whatever, and you have an instant low-fat 'mayonnaise'. Beancurd dressings have a very high protein value and are cheap to make. Here is a basic dressing.*

*6 oz (175 g) fresh beancurd, drained*
*1 tablespoon (15 ml) chopped onion*
*1 tablespoon (15 ml) olive oil or other vegetable oil*
*1 tablespoon (15 ml) water*
*1 teaspoon lemon juice*
*1 teaspoon honey*
*salt to taste*

Place all the ingredients in an electric blender. Blend together at high speed. Adjust seasoning.

PREPARATION TIME 5 MINUTES

## *Ginger and Soya Sauce Dressing*
MAKES 8 FL OZ (225 ML)

*This is a low-fat dressing. Serve it with lightly cooked vegetable salads, rice and bean*
*salads and root vegetable salads.*

*1 tablespoon (15 ml) peanut, sesame or other vegetable oil*
*1 tablespoon (15 ml) finely grated root ginger*
*4 fl oz (100 ml) shoyu (soya sauce)*
*4 fl oz (100 ml) water*
*1 tablespoon (15 ml) cider vinegar*
*1 clove garlic, crushed*

Combine the ingredients, mix well together and leave to stand for 15-20 minutes before serving.

PREPARATION TIME 5 MINUTES
STANDING TIME 15–20 MINUTES

## *Peanut Dressing*
MAKES 12 FL OZ (350 ML)

*Serve this dressing hot or at room temperature on cooked and uncooked vegetable*
*salads.*

*1 clove garlic, crushed*
*1 small onion, diced*
*1 tablespoon (15 ml) vegetable oil*
*4 oz (100 g) roasted (unsalted) peanuts or 4 oz (100 g) peanut butter*
*1 teaspoon brown sugar*
*1 tablespoon (15 ml) lemon juice*
*8 fl oz (225 ml) water*
*salt to taste*

Lightly brown the garlic and onion in the oil. Transfer the garlic, onion and frying oil to a blender and add all the other ingredients. Beat to a smooth mixture. Transfer the dressing to a pan, bring to the boil and then simmer over a low heat, stirring, for 5 minutes. Use immediately or allow to cool.

PREPARATION TIME 10 MINUTES

# VEGETABLES AND SAUCES

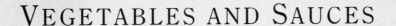

In a demivegetarian diet vegetables as an accompaniment or as a main course are just as important as chicken or fish dishes and the intrinsic qualities of each particular vegetable are appreciated and considered in the way they are cooked and presented. The best ways to cook vegetables in order to preserve their colour, texture and nutrient content are discussed in Cook's Notes (see p. 18).

Vegetables are important sources of vitamins, particularly vitamin C, minerals, carbohydrates and a major source of dietary fibre. Green vegetables contain small amounts of high-quality protein. Root vegetables such as potatoes, parsnips, swedes and turnips are the parts of the plants where energy is stored, and they thus provide a source of starches and natural sugars in our diets.

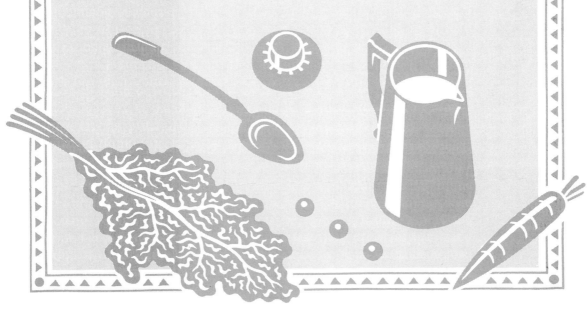

Good-quality vegetables, simply cooked and served on their own, are quite delicious enough to grace our tables, but they may also provide the basis for tasty and interesting main-course dishes. A selection of recipes for such dishes is given here. A collection of simple but versatile and flavoursome sauces is given at the end of the chapter. Some are recommended for particular recipes, but choose any one of them to go with any dish in the book which you feel would be enhanced by the addition of a sauce.

Raw vegetables should also play a role in the nutritional and culinary aspects of a demivegetarian (see Salads and Dressings, p. 59).

## *Parsnip Mousse with Toasted Almonds*

### SERVES 8

*This recipe freezes very well. When cooked, it should be allowed to cool before freezing. When needed, the mousse should be allowed to thaw and then reheated gently in a bain-marie in the oven. It is most attractively presented in individual moulds, but can also be made in one large one.*

*1¼ lb (550 g) parsnips, peeled*
*¼ pint (150 ml) milk*
*¼ pint (150 ml) cold water*
*½ teaspoon salt*
*4 oz (100 g) cream cheese*
*3 medium eggs*
*2 tablespoons (30 ml) dry sherry*
*grated nutmeg*
*½ oz (15 g) butter*
*1 oz (25 g) toasted flaked almonds*

Preheat the oven to 375° F (190° C, gas mark 5). Chop the parsnips roughly and bring them carefully to the boil with the milk, water and salt. Simmer carefully until just cooked. Remove from the heat and purée until very smooth. Then beat in the cream cheese, eggs, sherry and nutmeg. (This can be done very easily with a hand-held liquidizer.) Take eight individual ramekins and rub the insides with the butter. Divide the almonds among the bases. Alternatively, prepare a 1 pint (550 ml) pudding basin and line the base with the almonds. Spoon in the parsnip mixture. Place in the oven in a *bain-marie* and cook until set. Allow to cool for 5 minutes before turning out.

PREPARATION TIME 1 HOUR (INCLUDING UP TO 35 MINUTES BAKING TIME)

# Stir-Fried Vegetables

SERVES 4-6

*Stir-frying preserves the flavour and nutritional value of the vegetables. It is also a quick and versatile method of making a one-pot meal. Bite-sized pieces of cooked chicken, fish or beancurd can be added to the frying vegetables and just heated through before serving. Cooked grains can also be stirred in at the end. A wok is the best pan to use for stir-frying because its shape concentrates the heat on the food and cooks it quickly and evenly (assuming you stir continuously). Chop the vegetables into bite-sized pieces and add them to the wok in order according to their hardness. For example, add carrot before courgettes and courgettes before beansprouts.*
*Here is a general recipe for stir-fried vegetables. The ingredients can be changed according to what is available.*

*2 tablespoons (30 ml) vegetable oil*
*1 clove garlic, crushed*
*1 small onion, chopped*
*1 teaspoon grated root ginger or 1 teaspoon grated lemon peel*
*1½ lb (700 g) total weight washed and chopped vegetables.*
*Select one or more from:*
*beansprouts*
*cabbage, shredded*
*carrots, sliced*
*celery, chopped*
*courgettes, sliced*
*French or green beans, stringed and chopped*
*green or red peppers, seeded, cored and sliced*
*1 tablespoon (15 ml) soya sauce*

*Optional extras*
*cooked chicken*
*cooked filleted fish*
*omelette, cut into strips*
*beancurd, cut into cubes*
*peanuts or other nuts*
*sesame seeds, dry-roasted, or 2 tablespoons (15-30 ml) tahini*

Heat the oil in a wok and add the garlic, onion and ginger or lemon peel. Stir-fry to soften the onion. Add the vegetables (hardest first) and stir-fry until lightly cooked but still crunchy. Add the soya sauce and stir in the optional extras. Heat through and serve.

PREPARATION TIME 20 MINUTES

### Variation

For a hot chilli dish add ½-2 finely chopped fresh or dried chillies at the same time as the garlic and onion.

## Spiced Vegetable and Lentil Roast

SERVES 4

*Couscous gives this savoury dish a lovely light texture, but if it is not available, use
flour, breadcrumbs or, to give more body, any other grains (added with the lentils).*

*5 oz (150 g) red lentils, washed*
*1 medium onion, chopped*
*1 medium carrot, scrubbed and chopped*
*1 stick celery, scrubbed and chopped*
*½ teaspoon ground cumin*
*½ teaspoon ground coriander*
*¾ teaspoon ground turmeric*
*sea salt to taste*
*1 oz (25 g) couscous*
*½ teaspoon yeast extract*
*2 oz (50 g) wholemeal breadcrumbs*
*1 oz (25 g) vegetable margarine*

Put the lentils, onion, carrot, celery, cumin, coriander, turmeric and salt in a saucepan.
Just cover with water, bring to the boil, cover, and simmer for 30 minutes, stirring
occasionally. Sprinkle in the couscous and cook for a further 5 minutes. Preheat the oven
to 400° F (200° C, gas mark 6). Transfer the contents of the pan to an ovenproof dish or
casserole and spread the yeast extract over the mixture. Cover with breadcrumbs and
dot with margarine. Bake for 30-40 minutes in the hot oven.

PREPARATION TIME 1 HOUR 15 MINUTES

## Oden

SERVES 6-8

*A popular Japanese winter casserole, Oden is often prepared for festive occasions when
people help themselves out of the oden pot, which can bubble away all evening without
spoiling. In some big cities vendors sell oden in the streets. From experience I can tell
you vendors are not keen on customers who want to pick and choose from the oden pot.
They believe in pot luck.*

*2 pints (1.1 litres) stock*
*1 tablespoon (15 ml) sugar*
*1 tablespoon (15 ml) soya sauce*
*2 medium carrots, cut into 2 in (5 cm) pieces*
*8 oz (225 g) baby turnips or daikon, chopped*
*8 oz (225 g) new potatoes, scrubbed*
*12 oz (350 g) pressed beancurd, cut into 2 in (5 cm) pieces*
*6 hard-boiled eggs, shelled*
*salt to taste*

Bring the stock to the boil in a large pot and add the sugar and soya sauce. Add the carrots, turnips or daikon and potatoes, and simmer, covered, for 15 minutes. Add the beancurd, cabbage, whole hard-boiled eggs and salt. Simmer, covered, for another 15 minutes or until all the vegetables are tender. Transfer the *oden* to a warmed tureen and serve.

PREPARATION TIME 45 MINUTES

## *Moroccan Vegetable Casserole with Couscous*
### SERVES 6

*No two casseroles need be the same and the vegetables used in this recipe may be altered according to what is available or in season. The cooking method is, however, interesting. The Moroccans add the vegetables straight to boiling water and do not sauté them first. Towards the end of the cooking period onions and seasonings are fried together and added to the pot. The casserole develops an unexpectedly good flavour and goes very well with couscous. In North Africa the preparation of couscous is attended by its own tradition (see p. 138), but it can be cooked very simply if you wish. Put the couscous in a bowl, cover it with hot water and leave it to stand for 15 minutes. Meanwhile chop up some fresh herbs – coriander, mint or parsley, for example. Drain the couscous in a colander, mix in the fresh herbs, a little salt and it is ready.*

*2 pints (1.1 litres) water*
*2 teaspoons salt*
*4-6 cloves garlic, peeled*
*2 medium carrots, peeled and chopped*
*2 medium onions, diced*
*2 medium potatoes, peeled and chopped*
*1 small turnip, peeled and chopped*
*2 medium courgettes, thickly sliced*
*1 medium aubergine, cubed*
*4 tablespoons (60 ml) vegetable oil*
*1-2 chilli peppers, seeded and chopped*
*1 teaspoon ground cumin*
*2 tablespoons (30 ml) chopped parsley*
*1 lb (450 g) couscous (cooked as above)*

Put the water and salt in a large pot and bring to the boil. Add the next seven ingredients, reserving half the diced onion. Cover and return to the boil, reduce the heat and simmer until all the vegetables are tender. Heat the oil in a heavy frying pan and sauté the reserved onion, chilli peppers, cumin and parsley until the onion is soft. Pour this mixture into the vegetable pot and simmer for a further 5 minutes. With a slotted spoon lift out some of the vegetables and use them to garnish the couscous. Serve the couscous and casserole from central dishes.

PREPARATION TIME 45 MINUTES

## Potato and Artichoke Purée with Roasted Pine Nuts
### SERVES 6

*This has a refined, subtle flavour which is best complemented by a plain dish such as roast chicken or grilled fish. This recipe can be prepared an hour or so in advance and reheated in the oven in a covered dish.*

*1½ lb (675 g) floury potatoes, peeled and chopped*
*6 oz (175 g) Jerusalem artichokes, peeled and halved*
*3 oz (75 g) butter*
*5 oz (150 ml) single cream*
*milk if necessary*
*salt (add very carefully)*
*1 oz (25 g) toasted pine nuts*

Cook the potatoes in lightly salted water. Meanwhile cook the artichokes separately in more lightly salted water. When both vegetables are cooked, drain them well and return them to one of the pans to dry out over a low heat for a minute or so. They must be stirred constantly so as not to burn. Then remove them from the heat, mash them together, adding the butter and the cream while they are still hot. A very smooth texture should be obtained and this can be achieved either by pressing the mixture through a sieve or by processing at a low speed with a hand-held liquidizer. Some milk can be added to obtain the consistency of thick cream. Serve with the toasted pine nuts scattered over the top.

PREPARATION TIME 30 MINUTES

## Vegan Vegetable Pasties
### SERVES 6

*The vegetables given here are only suggestions; use others more to your taste or more easily available if you wish. Serve on their own with salad or, for a non-vegan dish, topped with a cheese sauce and accompanied by boiled grains.*

*1 large potato, scrubbed or peeled and diced*
*1 large carrot, scrubbed or peeled and diced*
*4 oz (100 g) fresh peas or defrosted frozen peas*
*4 oz (100 g) French beans, topped, tailed, stringed and chopped*
*1 lb (450 g) wholemeal shortcrust pastry*
*½ teaspoon miso*
*2 tablespoons (30 ml) boiling water*
*2 tablespoons (30 ml) chopped parsley*
*2 fl oz (50 ml) milk*

Put the potato and carrot into a pan and barely cover with water. Bring to the boil and cook for 6-8 minutes. Add the peas and beans and simmer until all the vegetables are tender. Drain, rinse the cooked vegetables under cold water and set aside.

Preheat the oven to 350° F (180° C, gas mark 4). Roll out the pastry thinly (about ¼ in/5 mm) and cut into 6 in (15 cm) rounds.

Dissolve the miso in the boiling water, add the cooked vegetables and parsley and mix well together. Put a dessertspoonful of this mixture on the centre of each pastry round. Fold the rounds into half-moon shapes and press the edges together, using water to help them stick if necessary. Brush the top of each half-moon with milk, put the pasties on a lightly greased baking tray and bake in the preheated oven for 15 minutes.

PREPARATION TIME 1 HOUR

# Vegetables, Apples and Peanuts with Potato Cheese Topping
SERVES 4

*This recipe neatly combines several different food groups to give a nutritious and distinctive main course dish.*

1 lb (450 g) potatoes
6 oz (175 g) Cheddar cheese, grated
1 egg, beaten
2 fl oz (50 ml) milk
salt and freshly ground black pepper
2 tablespoons (30 ml) vegetable oil
2 medium onions, finely chopped
2 large carrots, quartered lengthwise and cut thinly across
4 oz (100 g) celery, finely chopped
1 large cooking apple, peeled, cored and chopped
8 oz (225 g) peanuts
½ teaspoon cayenne
1 teaspoon turmeric

Boil the potatoes in their skins until tender. Drain, rinse them under cold water and peel off the skins. Mash the potatoes and stir in half the cheese, the egg and milk, and season with salt and black pepper. Beat the mixture smooth. Preheat the oven to 375° F (190° C, gas mark 5). Heat the oil in a large saucepan and add the onions, carrots, celery and apple. Stir well and cook over a medium heat until lightly browned. Add the peanuts, cayenne, turmeric and a little more salt and black pepper, and cook, stirring, for a further 1-2 minutes. Put the vegetable mixture into a baking dish and cover with the potato and cheese mixture. Sprinkle the remaining cheese on top and bake in the preheated oven for 30 minutes.

PREPARATION TIME 1 HOUR

## Stuffed Aubergines Vegan Style
### SERVES 4

*Demivegetarianism is based on a balanced mixed diet and thus there is good reason to
be eclectic in choosing recipes. Vegans do not eat any foods containing animal products.
They are vegetarians minus dairy foods. Their diet is very low in fat and the occasional
vegan recipe fits well into a demivegetarian diet. In this recipe for stuffed aubergines a
small amount of miso is included in the ingredients. Miso is one of the few non-animal
foods which contain the essential vitamin B12.
Serve with broccoli, spinach or other greens. For a substantial meal serve with rice, a
sauce and greens.*

2 medium-sized aubergines
1 tablespoon (15 ml) vegetable oil
2 large onions, chopped
2 cloves garlic, crushed
6 oz (175 g) mushrooms, chopped
4 large tomatoes, skinned and chopped
1 teaspoon miso paste
3 oz (75 g) wholemeal breadcrumbs
1 oz (25 g) wheatgerm
4 oz (100 g) blanched almonds, chopped
1 tablespoon (15 ml) chopped parsley
1 teaspoon lemon juice
salt and black pepper

Preheat the oven to 350° F (180° C, gas mark 4). Prick the aubergines four or five times
each with a fork to prevent them from bursting. Place them on a lightly greased baking
tray and bake for 30 minutes in the preheated oven, turning once. Leave the oven on. Cut
the aubergines in half lengthways and scoop out most of the flesh but leave solid walls.
Chop the flesh. Heat the oil in a pan and fry the onions over a moderate heat for 3
minutes, stirring occasionally. Add the garlic, mushrooms, tomatoes and miso. Simmer
the mixture for 5 minutes and then add the aubergine flesh, breadcrumbs and
wheatgerm, half the almonds, the parsley and the lemon juice. Season to taste with salt
and black pepper and simmer for a further 2-3 minutes. Fill the aubergine shells with the
mixture. Put them on the baking tray, top with the remaining almonds and bake in the hot
oven for 20-25 minutes.

PREPARATION TIME 1 HOUR

## Lasagne Covent Garden
### SERVES 4–6

*This dish is a nutritious mixture and contains an excellent balance of proteins,
vitamins, minerals and carbohydrates. The fat content is low.*

12 oz (350 g) carrots, peeled and sliced
12 oz (350 g) parsnips, peeled and sliced
½ oz (15 g) vegetable margarine
salt and freshly ground black pepper to taste
6 sheets wholemeal lasagne
12 oz (350 g) cottage cheese
2 oz (50 g) walnuts, roughly chopped
1½ lb (800 g) fresh spinach, thawed, drained well and chopped
¼ teaspoon ground nutmeg
4 oz (100 g) mozzarella cheese, sliced thinly

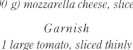

Garnish
1 large tomato, sliced thinly
fresh or dried basil

Preheat the oven to 350° F (180° C, gas mark 4). Cook the carrots in a large saucepan, containing enough boiling salted water to cover, for 5 minutes, then add the parsnips and continue cooking for a further 10 minutes or until both vegetables are very tender. Drain the vegetables well and mash together with the margarine and season with salt and pepper. Spread the mixture over the base of an ovenproof dish. Cover it with three sheets of the lasagne (uncooked), then with the cottage cheese mixed with the chopped walnuts. Cover this layer with the remaining lasagne. Spread over this the spinach seasoned with nutmeg, salt and pepper. Place the cheese slices over the top and bake in the preheated oven for 30 minutes or until the lasagne is tender and the cheese golden brown. Remove from the oven and decorate with slices of tomato and fresh basil.

PREPARATION TIME 1 HOUR 15 MINUTES (INCLUDING 30 MINUTES BAKING TIME)

## *Jerusalem Artichokes, Greens and Garlic*
SERVES 4 AS A SIDE DISH

*Use Jerusalem artichokes in season; they are a lovely vegetable and a nice change from potatoes.*

3 cloves garlic, crushed
2 tablespoons (30 ml) vegetable oil
8 oz (225 g) Jerusalem artichokes, scrubbed, knobs cut off, sliced
4 oz (100 g) greens (broccoli, kale, spinach, etc.) or sprout tops, chopped
soya sauce to taste

Sauté the garlic in the vegetable oil in a pan for 1 minute. Add the Jerusalem artichokes and cook, stirring, for about 7 minutes over a moderate heat, adding a little water if necessary to prevent browning. Add the greens and cook for a further 5 minutes. Season to taste with soya sauce and serve immediately.

PREPARATION TIME 25 MINUTES

## Thai Curried Beancurd With Vegetables

SERVES 4

*The vegetables given in this recipe are only suggestions and any suitable combination available may be used. This recipe, unlike most Thai curries, does not use coconut milk and thus is a little quicker and simpler to prepare. Serve with rice.*

*3 tablespoons (45 ml) vegetable oil*
*2 tablespoons (30 ml) curry powder mixed to a paste with 2 tablespoons (30 ml) white*
*vinegar and 2 tablespoons (30 ml) water*
*8 oz (225 g) beancurd, pressed and cut into 1 in (2.5 cm) cubes*
*2 tablespoons (30 ml) soya sauce*
*1 teaspoon grated lemon rind or chopped lemon grass*
*4 oz (100 g) green beans, cut into 2 in (5 cm) lengths*
*4 oz (100 g) cauliflower, cut into florets*
*4 oz (100 g) cabbage or Chinese cabbage, coarsely shredded*
*4 oz (100 g) fresh mushrooms, sliced*
*2 teaspoons sugar*
*coriander or mint or parsley leaves, finely chopped, to garnish*

Heat the oil in a large pan or wok and stir-fry the curry paste for 3-4 minutes. Add the beancurd, soya sauce and lemon rind or grass and continue to stir-fry for a further 6-7 minutes. Add the green beans, cauliflower, cabbage and mushrooms. Cook, stirring, until they are tender enough to eat but still retain some bite (about 4-5 minutes). Stir in the sugar and serve garnished with fresh herbs.

PREPARATION TIME 35 MINUTES

## Japanese Spicy Aubergines

SERVES 4

*Serve as a side dish.*

*4 tablespoons (60 ml) vegetable oil*
*1 lb (450 g) aubergines cut into ¾ in (2 cm) cubes, salted, pressed, rinsed and*
*drained*
*2 teaspoons finely grated root ginger*
*1 clove garlic, crushed*
*1 medium onion, finely sliced*
*pinch cayenne pepper or Japanese seven-spice powder*
*3 fl oz (75 ml) vegetable stock or water*
*1 teaspoon sugar*
*1 tablespoon (15 ml) finely chopped chives or parsley or 1 sheet nori seaweed,*
*toasted or crumbled, to garnish*

▼▼▼▼▼▼▼▼▼▼▼▼▼▼▼▼▼▼▼▼▼▼▼▼▼▼▼▼▼▼▼▼▼▼▼

Heat the oil in a heavy pan, add the aubergines and sauté for 3-4 minutes. Stir frequently. Remove the aubergines from the pan, drain, and reserve the oil. Put the aubergines to one side and return the oil to the pan. Add the ginger, garlic, onion and cayenne or seven-spice powder and sauté over a high flame for 30 seconds. Reduce the heat, add the stock and sugar, and mix well. Add the aubergines and bring to the boil. Turn off the heat and serve garnished with chives, parsley or nori.

PREPARATION TIME 20 MINUTES (PLUS 30 MINUTES
TO SALT THE AUBERGINES)

▼▼▼▼▼▼▼▼▼▼▼▼▼▼▼▼▼▼▼▼▼▼▼▼▼▼▼▼▼▼▼▼▼▼▼

# Rosemary Vegetable Crumble
## SERVES 4-6

*This rich, rosemary-flavoured vegetable dish is guaranteed to satisfy the hungry and those who enjoy good food. It is also suitable for vegans.*

*2 onions, chopped*
*2 teaspoons chopped fresh rosemary or 1 teaspoon dried rosemary*
*2 tablespoons (30 ml) vegetable oil*
*2 carrots, scrubbed and cut into large chunks*
*2 sticks celery, coarsely chopped*
*1 large potato, peeled and cut into large chunks*
*1 small turnip, peeled and cut into large chunks*
*1 small swede, peeled and cut into large chunks*
*8 oz (225 g) mushrooms, chopped*
*8 oz (225 g) tomatoes, peeled and chopped*
*¼ small cauliflower, cut in large florets*
*1 tablespoon (15 ml) miso*

### Topping
*6 oz (175 g) wholemeal flour*
*2 oz (50 g) rolled oats*
*3 oz (75 g) margarine*
*1 oz (25 g) sunflower seeds*
*salt*

Preheat the oven to 400° F (200° C, gas mark 6). Sauté the onions and rosemary in the oil in a large saucepan for 5 minutes. Add the rest of the vegetables, cover, and cook for 15 minutes, adding a little water if necessary to prevent browning. At the end of this time use a little of the juice from the pan to dissolve the miso and stir it into the vegetables. Remove the pan from the heat. Make the crumble by rubbing the margarine into the flour and oats until you have formed a crumb-like mixture. Add to this the sunflower seeds and salt to taste. Put the cooked vegetables into a casserole dish or tray and cover them with the crumble mix. Bake in the hot oven for 20 minutes or until nicely browned.

# Aloo *Curry with Chapattis*

### SERVES 4-6

*Aloo in an Indian menu means potato. The* aloo *curry given here is simple to prepare
and unexpectedly tasty. Serve it as a vegetarian main course with Saffron Rice
(see p. 137) or chapattis (see below).*

*2 medium tomatoes*
*3 tablespoons (45 ml) vegetable oil*
*1 teaspoon turmeric*
*1 teaspoon cumin seeds*
*½ teaspoon crushed coriander seeds or ground coriander*
*½ teaspoon cayenne pepper*
*1 lb (45 g) potatoes, sliced*
*1 teaspoon salt*
*14 fl oz (400 ml) hot water*
*5 oz (150 ml) natural yoghourt*

Pour boiling water over the tomatoes; leave for 10 seconds, then skin them and chop the
flesh. In a heavy saucepan, heat the oil gently and cook the turmeric, cumin, coriander
and cayenne pepper, stirring, for 2 minutes. Add the potatoes and stir gently until they
are completely coated with the spices. Cook for 5 minutes, stirring often. Add the salt
and the chopped tomatoes and cook for 2-3 minutes. Add the hot water, bring to the boil,
then reduce the heat and simmer uncovered for 20 minutes or until the potatoes are
tender. Either add the yoghourt to the curry, stir, heat through and serve, or serve the
curry and the yoghourt in separate bowls.

### PREPARATION TIME 50 MINUTES

# *Chapattis*

### MAKES 8

*This Indian bread is normally eaten with curried foods and other Indian-style savoury
dishes.*

*8 oz (225 g) 100% wholewheat flour*
*2 tablespoons (30 ml) vegetable oil*
*½ teaspoon salt*
*6 fl oz (175 ml) warm water*

Mix the flour, oil, salt and warm water in a bowl to form a fairly stiff dough that comes
away from the side of the bowl. Knead the dough until the texture is smooth and elastic.
Leave it to rest for 30-60 minutes. Divide it into eight even-sized portions and roll them
into balls. Flatten the balls on a floured board and roll them out thinly into circles
approximately 8 in (20 cm) in diameter. Heat an ungreased heavy frying pan over a high
flame. Place a chapatti in the pan and cook for about 1 minute. Turn the chapatti over and

press the edges with a spatula; they should puff up slightly. Continue cooking until the underside is just mottled with brown spots. Remove the chapatti from the pan and store it in a heated oven or wrap in a clean cloth to keep it warm while you cook the others.

PREPARATION TIME 45 MINUTES-1 HOUR (INCLUDING 30 MINUTES-1 HOUR RESTING TIME FOR THE DOUGH)

# Stir-Fried Sesame Mangetout
SERVES 4

*1 tablespoon (15 ml) sesame oil*
*½ medium red pepper, seeded and cut into very fine strips about 2 in (5 cm) long*
*2 teaspoons finely grated root ginger*
*8 oz (225 g) mangetout peas, topped and tailed*
*2 teaspoons sesame seeds*

Heat the sesame oil over a medium heat in a wok or a heavy-bottomed frying pan. Add the red pepper and the ginger. Stir with a wooden spoon and, as soon as the pepper strips start to soften, add the mangetout and sesame seeds. Continue to cook for 2 minutes, stirring constantly. Serve immediately.

PREPARATION TIME 15 MINUTES

# Sauces
# Tahini Sauce
MAKES 10 FL OZ (300 ML)

*This sauce is excellent just on its own with bread or as a salad dressing. Also serve it with rice and vegetable dishes.*

*2 cloves garlic, crushed*
*salt*
*4 fl oz (100 ml) tahini*
*4 fl oz (100 ml) water*
*juice of 2 lemons*

Combine the garlic, salt and tahini in a blender and beat until smooth. Add the water and lemon juice and blend in. For a thicker or thinner sauce use less or more water and lemon juice respectively.

PREPARATION TIME 5 MINUTES

### Variation
Add 4 fl oz (100 ml) natural yoghourt to the tahini sauce for a thicker, sharper-flavoured sauce.

# Béchamel Sauce
MAKES ABOUT 14 FL OZ (400 ML)

*1 oz (25 g) butter*
*2 tablespoons (30 ml) finely diced onion*
*1 oz (25 g) wholemeal flour*
*10 fl oz (275 ml) milk*
*bay leaf*
*pinch nutmeg*
*salt and freshly ground black pepper to taste*

Melt the butter in a heavy saucepan over a low heat. Add the onion and sauté until soft and transparent. Stir in the flour to form a smooth paste and cook, stirring, for 2-3 minutes. Add the milk slowly to the pan, stirring constantly. Continue cooking and stirring until the sauce thickens. Add the bay leaf, nutmeg and salt and black pepper and simmer, covered, over a very low heat for 10 minutes. Stir occasionally.

PREPARATION TIME 20 MINUTES

### Variation
Stir 2 oz (50 g) grated Cheddar cheese or other suitable cheese into the cooked béchamel sauce until it has melted. For extra flavour also stir in 1 teaspoon prepared English mustard.

# Tomato Sauce
MAKES ABOUT 30 FL OZ (850 ML)

*2 oz (50 g) butter or vegetable oil*
*1 medium onion, finely diced*
*2 lb (900 g) tinned tomatoes, drained*
*4 cloves garlic, crushed*
*1 medium green pepper, seeded, cored and diced*
*2 teaspoons crushed oregano*
*2 tablespoons (30 ml) chopped fresh parsley*
*1 bay leaf*
*salt and pepper*

Melt the butter or heat the oil in a heavy saucepan and fry the onions over a low heat until soft. Chop the tomatoes into small pieces and add them, with the garlic and green pepper, to the onions, stir well, and simmer for 10 minutes. Add the herbs and season to taste with salt and black pepper. Simmer for a further 10 minutes. Use immediately or allow to cool.

PREPARATION TIME 30 MINUTES

### Variation
For a thicker tomato sauce suitable for some types of pizza or to mix with stuffings for vegetables and pasta dishes, add 6 oz (175 g) tomato purée with the chopped tomatoes.

90

## Raw Tomato Sauce
MAKES 10 FL OZ (300 ML)

*Use good, fresh, ripe tomatoes. For a very quick sauce use tinned tomatoes instead of
fresh ones.*

*1 lb (450 g) ripe tomatoes, skinned and seeded
1 tablespoon (15 ml) wine vinegar
2 tablespoons (30 ml) olive oil
1 tablespoon (15 ml) finely chopped parsley
1 teaspoon dried oregano
salt and black pepper to taste*

Place all the ingredients in a liquidizer and blend at low speed until a smooth sauce is
obtained. Use the sauce on delicate vegetables, either as it is or thinned with whipping
cream.

PREPARATION TIME 10 MINUTES

## Green Sauce
MAKES 10 FL OZ (300 ML)

*This is a good, general-purpose sauce. You can use it on many hot or cold, young,
tender vegetables.*

*1 bunch of good fresh watercress, well washed
1 tablespoon (15 ml) vegetable oil
5 fl oz (150 ml) mayonnaise (see p. 72)
4 fl oz (100 ml) yoghourt
salt and pepper
watercress tips to garnish (optional)*

Trim the roots from the watercress and remove any discoloured leaves. Plunge the
trimmed watercress into a pan of well-salted boiling water for little more than 10 seconds.
(This may seem a minor step, but it greatly enhances the colour of the finished sauce.)
Drain and refresh the watercress under cold running water until it is quite chilled.
Squeeze the watercress free of any excess water, roughly chop it, place it in a liquidizer
with the oil and blend to a smooth purée. Mix the watercress purée, the mayonnaise and
the yoghourt together in a small mixing bowl. Season to taste with salt and pepper.

PREPARATION TIME 10 MINUTES

## Coriander Cream Sauce

MAKES 10 FL OZ (300 ML)

*A soft, mellow sauce that is good with eggs, pasta, salads and white fish.*

*1 bunch fresh coriander*
*5 oz (150 ml) single cream*
*4 tablespoons (60 ml) sunflower or peanut oil*
*2 tablespoons (30 ml) lemon juice*
*1 tablespoon (15 ml) French mustard*
*salt and black pepper to taste*

Wash the coriander well and shake it dry. Cut away all but the finest stems. Place the trimmed leaves in a blender. Add the rest of the ingredients and blend well at medium speed until a smooth green sauce is obtained. Adjust the seasoning.

PREPARATION TIME 5 MINUTES

## Uncooked Cream Sauce

MAKES 5 FL OZ (150 ML)

*This rich dressing can be stored for up to four days in the refrigerator. Try it on fresh young vegetables like carrots, broad beans, broccoli or new potatoes.*

*¼ pint (150 ml) chilled double cream*
*salt and cayenne pepper to taste*
*1-2 tablespoons (15-30 ml) wine vinegar*

Season the cream to taste with salt and cayenne pepper. Whip until it is nice and thick. Gradually stir in the vinegar to taste.

PREPARATION TIME 5 MINUTES

## Peanut Sauce

MAKES 12 FL OZ (350 ML)

*Serve this dressing hot or at room temperature on cooked and uncooked vegetable salads.*

*1 clove garlic, crushed*
*1 small onion, diced*
*1 tablespoon (15 ml) vegetable oil*
*4 oz (100 g) roasted (unsalted) peanuts or 4 oz (100 g) peanut butter*
*1 teaspoon brown sugar*
*1 tablespoon (15 ml) lemon juice*
*8 fl oz (225 g) water*
*salt to taste*

Lightly brown the garlic and onion in the oil. Transfer the garlic, onion and frying oil to a liquidizer or food processor and add all the other ingredients. Blend to a smooth mixture. Transfer the sauce to a pan, bring to the boil and then simmer over a low heat, stirring, for 5 minutes. Use immediately or at room temperature.

PREPARATION TIME 10 MINUTES

### Variation

For a spicy, hot peanut sauce in the Southeast Asian style, fry 1-2 seeded chopped red chillies with the garlic and onion.

## Speedy Chilli Sauce
MAKES 4 FL OZ (120 ML)

*This chilli dressing is fresh, hot and tangy. It is quick to make from products in the store cupboard. Use it on lightly cooked green beans, mangetout, cauliflower or broccoli.*

*2 tinned plum tomatoes, gently pressed free of juice*
*4 tablespoons (60 ml) vegetable oil*
*2 teaspoons hot pepper sauce*
*2 teaspoons natural soya sauce*

Pour all the ingredients into a small, steep-sided mixing bowl and beat together with a fork or a small wire whisk.

PREPARATION TIME 5 MINUTES

## Chinese Sweet and Sour Sauce with Tomato Purée
MAKES 12 FL OZ (350 ML)

*4 oz (100 g) sugar*
*4 fl oz (100 ml) wine vinegar*
*2 tablespoons (30 ml) soya sauce*
*2 tablespoons (30 ml) sherry*
*3 tablespoons (45 ml) tomato purée or ketchup*
*1 tablespoon (15 ml) cornflour dissolved in 4 fl oz (100 ml) water or pineapple juice*

Put the sugar, vinegar, soya sauce, sherry and tomato purée or ketchup in a heavy saucepan. Mix well and bring to the boil. Add the cornflour mixture. Stir constantly until the sauce thickens.

PREPARATION TIME 10 MINUTES

# Chinese Sweet and Sour Sauce with Ginger

MAKES 12 FL OZ (350 ML)

*1 tablespoon (15 ml) finely chopped fresh root ginger*
*4 oz (100 g) sugar*
*4 fl oz (100 ml) wine vinegar*
*6 tablespoons (90 ml) water or pineapple juice*
*1 tablespoon (15 ml) sherry*
*1½ tablespoons (25 ml) cornflour dissolved in 4 tablespoons (60 ml) water*

Using a garlic press, squeeze the juice from the root ginger into a heavy saucepan. Add the sugar, vinegar, water or pineapple juice and sherry. Bring to the boil and stir in the cornflour mixture to thicken.

PREPARATION TIME 10 MINUTES

# FISH

Because we live on an island the British have always been a
fish-eating people, but until quite recently there has been
a slow decline in the popularity of fish and consequent
reductions in our fishing fleets and the number of fishmongers on the high streets. Nowadays, with greater public
awareness of the health advantages of eating more fish and less meat
and of the many exciting but simple ways of cooking it, this trend has
been reversed. Supermarkets, fishmongers and frozen food outlets
now stock an even wider variety of fish than they did before the
decline and in this they are to be encouraged.

When buying fish choose either very fresh specimens or fish that
has been frozen fresh, immediately after it has been caught. Fish that
is neither sold fresh nor frozen but which has been stored on ice for a
few days is to be avoided. Fresh fish has firm flesh, shining scales
firmly attached to the body, clear eyes and almost no smell.

In Cook's Notes (see p. 26) the nutritional value of fish and the
basic methods of cooking it are discussed. The recipes I have chosen

▼▼▼▼▼▼▼▼▼▼▼▼▼▼▼▼▼▼▼▼▼▼▼▼▼▼▼▼▼▼▼▼▼▼▼

for this chapter are imaginative but simple and illustrate each of the main cooking methods for fish. Most of them specify a particular type of fish, but one of the advantages of cooking with fish is that different varieties may be used in the same recipe. Cooking times remain the same if you use the same weight of fish each time. For example, if a recipe stipulates a small whole fish, then you can substitute fillets or steaks or a larger fish or vice versa. Alternatively, you can adjust cooking times in accordance with the weight of the fish. Cooking methods are also interchangeable, and fish which can be grilled or barbecued may also be baked or fried. In fact, fish recipes are flexible and made for improvisation. Equally, if you do not wish to follow any recipe, then simply cook the whole fish or fillet or fish steak on its own using one of the basic methods described in Cook's Notes. Serve it unadorned with vegetables or a salad or with perhaps a hint of flavouring from lemon juice, garlic, olive oil, freshly chopped herbs or a homemade dressing such as mayonnaise or tahini sauce. Alternatively, marinate the fish in olive oil and lemon juice or grated root ginger and soya sauce and then cook it gently.

▼▼▼▼▼▼▼▼▼▼▼▼▼▼▼▼▼▼▼▼▼▼▼▼▼▼▼▼▼▼▼▼▼▼▼

## *Barbecued or Grilled Fish*

General methods for whole fish and fish kebabs are described below. Specific methods for specific fish are given in the individual recipes.

Grilling over a charcoal or wood fire is a delicious way to cook fish. Different techniques are used in different countries, but an ordinary picnic charcoal grill is perfectly suitable, and at second best, but still giving good results, a stove grill. Any type of fish can be used. Firmer fish can be grilled whole or cubed, marinated and skewered. Softer fish should be left whole.

For four people use 2-3 lb cod, trout, salmon, plaice, tuna, mackerel, red or grey mullet, sea bass or bream, or herring, either whole or filleted, cut into pieces and skewered. Serve barbecued whole fish or fish kebabs with lemon wedges, olives, a salad and lots of hot pitta bread.

### *Method for whole fish*

Wash and gut the fish, rinse and wipe them dry. Slit the skin diagonally on both sides in two or three places. This prevents the skin from splitting and allows the heat to penetrate. The scales are left on – they help to keep the flesh intact and moist. Sprinkle the fish with salt, brush with oil inside and out, and, if you wish, stuff the cavity with crushed garlic and fresh herbs such as coriander, basil, oregano or fennel. Oil the grill and heat it. Lay the fish on the grill and cook them over the glowing embers until they are tender and flaky. Turn them once during cooking. Try to adjust the cooking time and heat so that you get a fish with a soft moist interior and crispy brown skin.

To cook the fish under a domestic grill, oil a piece of aluminium foil and place it over the wire sheet of your grill pan. Place the fish on the top and cook under a moderate grill about 3-5 in (8-12 cm) away from the flame for 5-7 minutes each side (depending on the size of the fish).

*Top right: Preparation of Grilled 'Swimming' Fish – Mackerel (page 98)*
*Left and bottom right: Baked Red Mullet (page 97)*

*Top: Fried Chicken Balinese Style (page 126)*
*Bottom: Chinese Chicken with Walnuts (page 116) and Millet (page 21)*

*Method for skewered fish*

Fillet the fish and cut it into cubes. Make a marinade of equal amounts of olive oil and lemon juice seasoned with salt and black pepper, and marinate the fish in it for 1-2 hours. If they are available, add chopped fresh herbs to the marinade. Skewer the fish cubes, oil the grill and lay the skewers on it. Cook the kebabs over the glowing embers, frequently brushing them with marinade or oil.

To cook the kebabs under a domestic grill, place them under a moderate grill and cook for about 10 minutes, turning the skewers every now and again and basting with the marinade or oil if the marinade runs out.

# Baked Red Mullet in Fennel Sauce

## SERVES 4

*Red mullet are small, bright-red fish, at their best cooked whole by frying, grilling or baking. Mullet is generally eaten with the liver left intact and just the gut and scales removed. This recipe may also be prepared with mackerel or herring (cleaned and gutted).*

*4 × 8 oz (225 g) red mullet*
*salt and black pepper to taste*
*1 lemon, thinly sliced*
*1 medium bulb fennel, chopped (reserve the green fennel sprigs)*
*1 medium onion, chopped*
*2 tablespoons (30 ml) vegetable oil*
*1½ tablespoons (20 ml) flour*
*¾ pint (450 ml) fish stock or water*
*2 bay leaves*
*2 tablespoons (30 ml) lemon juice*

Preheat oven to 375° F (190° C, gas mark 5). Cut four pieces of aluminium foil big enough to wrap each fish and oil them lightly. Place each fish on a piece of foil, lightly season it with salt and black pepper, place two rings of lemon and a sprig of fennel on top and wrap the foil round it. Place the fish on a baking sheet in the oven and bake for 15-20 minutes or until the flesh just comes away from the bones. Meanwhile in a saucepan sauté the onion and fennel in the oil until well softened. Stir in the flour, cook for 1-2 minutes and then pour in the stock or water and add the bay leaves. Bring to the boil, reduce heat, season with salt and black pepper, cover the pan and simmer for 15 minutes, stirring occasionally. Remove the bay leaves, pour the sauce into a liquidizer and blend until smooth. Return it to the pan, stir in the lemon juice, heat through. Arrange the fish on individual plates, pour a little sauce over each and garnish with chopped fennel sprigs. Serve the remaining sauce in a separate bowl.

PREPARATION TIME 40 MINUTES

## Grilled 'Swimming' Fish

SERVES 4

*The most popular Japanese method of cooking fish is to grill them. Great care is taken to retain the shape of the fish during grilling, and to accomplish this the fish are stitched with skewers before cooking. For 'swimming' fish the skewer is pushed right through the fish at a point just below the head; it is then pushed back through the other side near the centre of the body and then finally out again near the tail.*

*4 × 8 oz (225 g) mackerel or herring, cleaned but with the heads left on*
*soya sauce (preferably* shoyu)
*1 lemon, thinly sliced*
*1½ tablespoons (25 ml) finely grated fresh root ginger*

Skewer the fish as described above and brush them with soya sauce. Preheat a moderate grill. Grill the fish for 5-8 minutes each side depending on the size of the fish. Perfectly grilled fish remains moist and the flesh will just come away from the bones. Turn the fish two or three times during cooking and each time brush with soya sauce. Remove the skewers and serve the fish hot, garnished with sliced lemon and grated ginger root.

PREPARATION TIME 30 MINUTES

### Variation

For very flavoursome fish marinate them in the following mixture for 1 hour before skewering and grilling. Brush them with the marinade during grilling.

*4 fl oz (100 ml) saké or white wine*
*4 fl oz (100 ml) naturally fermented soya sauce (*shoyu)
*1 tablespoon (15 ml) sugar*
*1 clove garlic, crushed*

Combine the ingredients in a small pan. Bring to the boil, remove from the heat and the marinade is ready.

## Chilli Hot Halibut

SERVES 4

*Halibut is a large flat fish with firm flesh of fine texture. It has a distinctive flavour that survives strong seasoning.*

*3 tablespoons (45 ml) vegetable oil*
*1 medium onion, finely chopped*
*½-1 red or green chilli pepper, seeded and finely chopped*
*1 teaspoon curry powder*
*½ teaspoon cumin seeds*
*2 tablespoons (30 ml) lemon juice*
*4 × 8 oz (225 g) halibut steaks*
*salt and black pepper to taste*

Heat the oil in a small frying pan and fry the onion and chilli pepper until the onion is just softened. Stir in the curry powder and cumin seeds and fry a further 2-3 minutes. Remove the pan from the heat. Put the halibut steaks into a glass or ceramic bowl. Stir the lemon juice into the onion spice mixture and then pour it over the halibut. Cover the bowl and leave the fish to marinate for 1 hour or more. Preheat a moderate grill. Cover the wire shelf in the grill pan with aluminium foil and arrange the halibut steaks on top, together with any marinade sticking to them. Grill for about 10 minutes or until the fish is tender. Do not turn the steaks over but if they start to dry out brush them with any marinade remaining in the bowl.

PREPARATION TIME 1 HOUR 30 MINUTES (INCLUDING 1 HOUR
MARINATING TIME)

## *Monk Fish Kebabs*

### SERVES 4

*Monk fish is firm-fleshed and very good for barbecuing or grilling. Serve with pilav rice*
*(see p. 102).*

*1 lb (450 g) filleted monk fish, cut into ½ in (1.25 cm) cubes or squares*
*3 tablespoons (45 ml) olive oil*
*3 tablespoons (45 ml) lemon juice*
*1 teaspoon ground cumin*
*3-4 bay leaves*
*salt and black pepper to taste*
*1 lb (450 g) small tomatoes, halved*
*2 medium green or red peppers, seeded, deribbed and cut into 2 in (5 cm) squares*
*lemon wedges*

Put the fish cubes into a bowl. Combine the olive oil, lemon juice, cumin, bay leaves and seasoning, and mix well. Pour this over the fish and leave it to marinate for 1-2 hours. Skewer (one skewer per person) the fish pieces, tomato halves and pepper squares in an attractive pattern and place them on an oiled grill over glowing charcoal or under the domestic grill of a stove. Cook, turning the kebabs occasionally and basting them with marinade if they start to dry out. Total cooking time is about 10 minutes.

PREPARATION TIME 20 MINUTES (PLUS 1 HOUR TO MARINATE)

### *Variation*
Other fish with firm flesh such as herring, mackerel, cod or trout may be used in this recipe.

## Herring Stuffed with Brown Rice and Apple
### SERVES 4

*This is a low-fat, well-balanced, healthy and delicious recipe. Served with a fresh salad,*
*it makes a nutritionally complete meal.*

*1 tablespoon (15 ml) vegetable oil*
*1 small onion, finely chopped*
*1 green pepper, seeded and finely chopped*
*8 oz (225 g) cooking apples, peeled, cored and finely sliced*
*12 oz (350 g) cooked brown rice*
*1 teaspoon cinnamon*
*1 oz (25 g) walnuts, chopped*
*1 oz (25 g) sultanas*
*salt and black pepper*
*4 × 6-8 oz (175-225 g) herring fillets, skinned*

Preheat oven to 350° F (180° C, gas mark 4). Heat the oil in a frying pan and sauté the onion and pepper until softened. Add the apples and fry for 2-3 minutes. Stir in half the rice, the cinnamon, walnuts and sultanas. Mix well and season to taste with salt and black pepper. Remove from the heat and distribute the stuffing between the herrings. Spoon it onto the fish at the head end and then roll them up from head to tail and secure with cocktail sticks. Arrange the rolls in a shallow ovenproof dish. If there is too much stuffing, combine it with the remaining brown rice. Distribute the remaining rice around the stuffed fish and sprinkle with the apple juice. Cover the dish with aluminium foil and bake for 25 minutes.

PREPARATION TIME 45 MINUTES (WITH PRECOOKED BROWN RICE)

## Sole Food Pancakes
### SERVES 6

*This recipe is simpler than it looks although the method is rather long-winded. This is a*
*relatively rich dish and should be reserved for special occasions such as dinner parties.*

*Pancake batter*
*8 oz (225 g) plain flour*
*salt to taste*
*cayenne pepper to taste*
*2 eggs, beaten*
*20 fl oz (600 ml) milk*
*2 tablespoons (30 ml) vegetable oil*

▼ ▼ ▼ ▼ ▼ ▼ ▼ ▼ ▼ ▼ ▼ ▼ ▼ ▼ ▼ ▼ ▼ ▼ ▼ ▼ ▼ ▼ ▼ ▼ ▼ ▼ ▼ ▼ ▼

### Sauce

*2 oz (50 g) butter*
*2 oz (50 g) plain flour*
*20 fl oz (600 ml) milk*
*2 fl oz (50 ml) single cream*
*cayenne pepper to taste*
*salt and pepper to taste*
*freshly chopped parsley to garnish*

### Filling

*2 oz (50 g) butter*
*1 lb (450 g) sole, filleted*
*5 fl oz (150 ml) white wine*
*juice of ½ lemon*
*salt and pepper to taste*
*2 carrots, cut into thin strips*
*1 leek, cut into thin strips*
*1 stick of celery, cut into thin strips*
*6 oz (175 g) shelled prawns*

To make the batter, sift the flour, a pinch of salt and cayenne pepper into a large bowl and make a well in the centre. Add the eggs and half the milk and beat until smooth. Add the remaining milk and the oil, mix well, and leave for 30 minutes.

Heat an 8 in (20 cm) frying pan and wipe the inside with an oiled piece of kitchen paper. Pour in 2 tablespoons (30 ml) of the batter and tilt the pan so the butter covers the base. Cook until the underside is golden brown, then flip the pancake over and cook the other side. Continue to make pancakes until all the batter is used up, stacking them on top of each other with a piece of greaseproof paper between each pancake. Oil the pan lightly for each pancake.

To make the sauce, melt the butter in a saucepan, add the flour and cook gently, stirring, for 1 minute. Do not allow the roux to become discoloured. Gradually add the milk, stirring continuously until it has all been added and the sauce is smooth and thick. Add the cream and season with cayenne, salt and pepper. Keep the sauce warm over a very low light.

Preheat the oven to 350° F (180° C, gas mark 4). Using half the butter, grease a fireproof dish and lay the sole fillets in it. Pour the white wine over the fillets and season them with lemon juice, salt and pepper. Cover with buttered paper and bake for 15-20 minutes in the preheated oven. Add the juices from the fish to the prepared sauce. Melt the remaining butter in a saucepan, add the carrots, leek and celery, and cook gently over a low heat until tender. Combine the sole, vegetables, prawns and half the sauce together. Adjust the seasoning and spoon the mixture onto the pancakes. Roll up the pancakes and arrange them in a buttered baking dish. Pour the remaining sauce over the top and bake for 15 minutes. Sprinkle with parsley and serve immediately.

PREPARATION TIME 1 HOUR

▼▼▼▼▼▼▼▼▼▼▼▼▼▼▼▼▼▼▼▼▼▼▼▼▼▼▼▼▼▼▼▼▼▼▼▼

## *Fried Fish with Green Sauce (Salsa Verde)*
### SERVES 4

*Spain is surprisingly the world's third largest fish-eating nation. Spanish cooks are generally very good at cooking fish and Barcelona in particular has some of the best fish restaurants to be found anywhere. This recipe is quite simple but has a robust flavour. Serve the fish and sauce with plain boiled potatoes, a green salad in a lemon juice and olive oil dressing, and a bottle of decent Spanish white wine.*

*4 × 8 oz (225 g) steaks of cod, haddock, sole or other firm white fish*
*salt*
*1 tablespoon (15 ml) plain flour*
*3 tablespoons (45 ml) olive oil*
*1 medium onion, finely chopped*
*2 cloves garlic, crushed*
*2 fl oz (50 ml) white wine*
*3 tablespoons (45 ml) finely chopped parsley*
*juice of 1 lemon*

Preheat oven to 350° F (180° C, gas mark 4). Rinse the fish steaks and pat them dry. Season them lightly with salt, then sprinkle a little flour over both sides of each steak. Heat the oil in a frying pan and gently brown both sides of each steak but do not cook tender. Transfer the fish to a shallow ovenproof dish. Sauté the onion and garlic in the same oil until the onion is softened. Remove the pan from the heat and stir in the wine, parsley and lemon juice. Pour the contents of the pan over the fish steaks. Cover the top of the dish with aluminium foil and bake in the preheated oven for 15 minutes.

PREPARATION TIME 30 MINUTES

▼▼▼▼▼▼▼▼▼▼▼▼▼▼▼▼▼▼▼▼▼▼▼▼▼▼▼▼▼▼▼▼▼▼▼▼

## *Pilav Rice and Fish Casserole*
### SERVES 4–6

*This recipe is in two stages. First, a pilav rice, traditionally served with fish in the Middle East, is prepared. Secondly, the pilav rice is used in the preparation of the fish casserole. The pilav rice may, of course, be made on its own and used with other dishes.*

### *Pilav rice*
*The rice may, if it is convenient, be prepared well before the fish casserole.*

*4 tablespoons (60 ml) olive oil*
*½ teaspoon (2.5 ml) crushed saffron or 1 teaspoon (5 ml) turmeric*
*1 lb (450 g) long-grain white rice, washed and drained*
*salt and black pepper*
*2 oz (50 g) pine nuts or almonds, blanched*
*2 medium onions, sliced*

Heat half the oil in a heavy frying pan and stir in the saffron or turmeric. Measure out the rice in cupfuls and note how many there are. Stir the rice into the frying pan and fry, stirring until all the grains are coated with oil and tinted slightly yellow. Remove the pan from the heat. Pour into the pan boiling water equal to 1½ times the volume of rice. Season to taste with salt and pepper. Bring to the boil, reduce the heat, cover, and simmer for 20 minutes or until all the moisture is absorbed and the rice is tender. Meanwhile, fry the pine nuts in the remaining oil until they are lightly browned. Add the onions and stir-fry until they are softened. Serve the rice in a mound with the onions and pine nuts sprinkled over the top or set aside for use in the fish casserole.

*Pilav rice and fish casserole*
*1½ lb (700 g) firm white filleted fish*
*juice of 2 lemons*
*4 tablespoons (60 ml) olive oil*
*2 cloves garlic, crushed*
*2 tablespoons (30 ml) chopped fresh parsley*
*salt and black pepper*
*pilav rice, as prepared above*
*2 tablespoons (30 ml) pine nuts or almonds*

Preheat the oven to 180° C (350° F, gas mark 4). Put the fish in a baking dish. Combine the juice of 1 lemon, 2 tablespoons (30 ml) olive oil, the garlic, parsley and seasoning to taste and pour the mixture over the fish. Cover the dish and bake in the preheated oven for 15-20 minutes or until the fish is tender and flaky. Remove the fish and flake it into small pieces.

Make a bed of half the pilav rice in the same baking dish, cover it with half the fish and sprinkle with lemon juice. Repeat for another layer. In the remaining oil fry the pine nuts or almonds until they are light brown, and then pour the nuts and oil over the contents of the dish. Bake uncovered in the hot oven for 15 minutes.

COOKING TIME FOR THE PILAV RICE 25 MINUTES
COOKING TIME FOR THE CASSEROLE 45 MINUTES

## Baked Fish with Shiitake
### SERVES 4

*The Japanese method of baking fish is very simple and preserves the flavour of the fish. It was developed to make use of top burners because the Japanese do not normally use ovens. Cooked on top of the stove or in the oven, this is a complete and tasty dish.*

*4 dried shiitake (Japanese mushrooms) or 4 large fresh mushrooms*
*1 lb (450 g) filleted white fish*
*1 medium onion, sliced*
*2 medium green peppers, cored, seeded and quartered*
*salt and black pepper to taste*
*4 teaspoons saké or white wine*
*1 lemon, sliced*
*soya sauce to taste*

Soak the shiitake in cold water for 20 minutes. Cut away any hard stems and criss-cross the caps with shallow knife cuts. Alternatively, use fresh mushrooms with the stems removed. Cut the fish into four equal pieces and prepare pieces of aluminium foil 10 × 10 in (25 × 25 cm). Lightly grease the foil and, on each piece, lay in order a portion of onion slices, fish, green pepper and shiitake or mushrooms. Season with salt, pepper and saké or white wine, top with a piece of lemon and wrap the foil over the lot. Crimp the edges of the foil to ensure a tight seal. Preheat the frying pan over a moderate heat, place the wrapped fish in it, cover and cook for 10-12 minutes. Turn once or twice. Alternatively, bake the foil parcels in a preheated oven at 400° F (200° C, gas mark 6) for 20 minutes. Serve on individual plates and let the diners open the packets themselves. Season with soya sauce.

### PREPARATION AND COOKING TIME 50 MINUTES

*Variation*
Replace half the fish with white chicken meat cut into 1 in (2.5 cm) strips.

## Herring Simmered with Wine and Soya Sauce
### SERVES 4

*4 whole fresh herring, about 2 lb (900 g) in total weight*
*1 tablespoon (15 ml) honey*
*4 fl oz (100 ml) saké or dry white wine*
*2 fl oz (50 ml) soya sauce*
*2 in (5 cm) piece of fresh root ginger, peeled and grated*

### Garnish
*4 oz (100 g) French beans, parboiled in a little salted water, or,*
*4 oz (100 g) fresh or frozen garden peas, cooked until just tender*

Clean the herrings and remove the heads. In a wide pan bring the honey, saké, soya sauce and ginger to a gentle boil. Place the fish in the pan and return to a gentle boil. Reduce the heat and very gently simmer for 15 minutes or until the fish is tender and nearly all the liquid has been absorbed or evaporated. Carefully remove the fish to a large serving plate and serve them garnished with French beans or garden peas.

PREPARATION TIME 40 MINUTES

# Fried Fish in Tomato Sauce
### SERVES 4

*For this dish, which is adapted from a recipe from Iraq, herring has been suggested, but you could use 1½ lb (700 g) of fillets or steaks of cod, haddock, halibut or sole, or the same weight of whole mullet or bass. For an interesting North African version of the dish, see the recipe below.*

*2-3 lb (900-1400 g) herrings, cleaned and filleted*
*juice of 1 lemon*
*salt and black pepper to taste*
*1½ lb (700 g) fresh tomatoes*
*4 tablespoons (60 ml) olive oil or sunflower seed oil*
*2 medium onions, sliced*
*2 cloves garlic, crushed*
*1 teaspoon dried thyme*
*1 egg, beaten*
*plain flour*
*oil for frying*
*chopped parsley to garnish*

Cut the fish into two portions and sprinkle them with lemon juice, salt and pepper. Set them aside for 30 minutes. Plunge the fresh tomatoes into a pan of boiling water for 1 minute. Remove, allow to cool a little, then peel off the skins. Cut them in half, gently squeeze out and discard the seeds, and cut the flesh into pieces. Heat the oil in a pan and add the onions and garlic. Sauté, while stirring, until the onions are softened. Add the tomatoes, season to taste, and stir in the thyme. Cover the pan and simmer for 10-15 minutes. Dip the fish pieces in egg and lightly flour them. Fry them in ¼ in (7 mm) hot oil until browned on both sides and tender. Transfer them to a serving dish, cover them with the tomato sauce, and garnish with chopped parsley.

PREPARATION TIME 1 HOUR

### Variation
Put the fried fish in a baking dish, pour the sauce over the top, cover the dish and bake in a preheated oven at 250° F (130° C, gas mark ½) for 20 minutes.

## Fried Fish in Hot Courgette and Tomato Sauce
SERVES 4

*Proceed as in the recipe above, but add 1 lb (450 g) chopped courgettes and ½-1
teaspoon hot pepper sauce or harissa (see p. 138) with the tomatoes.*

PREPARATION TIME 1 HOUR

## Fried Fish with Yellow Rice
SERVES 4

*Fillets of any of the popular white or oily fish may be used in this recipe in which the fish
is flavoured with lemon juice and fried and the rice is lightly curried and cooked
in fish stock.*

4 × 8 oz (225 g) fish fillets (reserve the skin, bones, heads and tails)
juice of 2 lemons
salt and black pepper to taste
vegetable oil for shallow-frying
2 medium onions, finely chopped
1 teaspoon ground cumin
½ teaspoon turmeric
1 teaspoon curry powder (optional)
12 oz (350 g) uncooked white rice, washed and drained
lemon wedges

Sprinkle the fillets with lemon juice and seasoning and set aside. Put the bones, skin,
heads and tails of the fish in a pot with 1 pint (575 ml) of water, bring to the boil, reduce
the heat and simmer for 30 minutes. Strain off the liquid and reserve.

Fry the fish in hot shallow oil in a heavy frying pan until it is nicely browned on both
sides. Lift the fish from the pan and set it aside in a low oven to keep warm. In the same
pan fry the onions until they are lightly browned, and then stir in the cumin, turmeric and
curry powder if used. Stir in the rice and sauté it for a few minutes. Add the fish stock and
enough extra water to make up 1½ pints (900 ml) liquid. Season to taste with salt and
black pepper. Bring to the boil, reduce the heat, cover, and simmer until the rice is
tender (about 15 minutes). Add more water if the pan dries out.

To serve, pile the rice on a serving dish with the fish fillets on top, and garnish with
lemon wedges.

PREPARATION TIME 50 MINUTES

# Thai Turbot and Vegetable Curry

## SERVES 4

*A specific type of fish and specific combination of vegetables are given in the recipe, but almost any type of filleted fish may be used and whatever combination of vegetables you like. The method is simple and good for improvisation. For a hot curry, use more curry powder than given in the recipe: for a milder one, use less. Serve with boiled rice.*

1½ lb (700 g) filleted turbot cut into large bite-sized pieces (reserve the bones, head and tail)
2 tablespoons (30 ml) vegetable oil
2 cloves garlic, crushed
½ medium onion, finely chopped
½ pint (300 ml) fish stock
2 teaspoons curry powder
2 tablespoons (30 ml) lemon juice
2 tablespoons (30 ml) fish sauce or soya sauce
1½ lb (700 g) mixed vegetables comprising:
green beans, cut into 2 in (5 cm) lengths
cauliflower, cut into small florets
Chinese cabbage, coarsely shredded
fresh mushrooms, sliced
tinned bamboo shoots, sliced
finely chopped coriander leaves to garnish

Put the bones, head and tail from the filleted fish into a saucepan, add ½ pint (300 ml) water, and simmer, covered, for 30 minutes. Drain off the stock and reserve it for use in the recipe.

Heat the oil in a saucepan or wok and sauté the garlic and onion until golden. Add the fish and stock and bring to the boil. Reduce the heat and simmer, uncovered, for 5 minutes. With a slotted spoon, lift out about a third of the fish chunks and transfer them to a blender. Add 4 fl oz (100 ml) of liquid from the pan, the curry powder, lemon juice and fish sauce. Blend until smooth and return the mixture to the pan. Add the vegetables to the pan, leaving those with a short cooking time to the last, and simmer uncovered until they are tender (about 10 minutes). Garnish with coriander leaves and serve.

PREPARATION TIME 1 HOUR (30 MINUTES IF COCONUT MILK IS USED
IN PLACE OF FISH STOCK)

### Variation

Replace the fish stock with canned coconut milk. Follow the same method but do not allow the coconut milk to boil.

## Thai Style Fish Cakes

SERVES 4

*1 lb (450 g) white fish fillets skinned*
*4 fl oz (100 ml) canned coconut milk or natural yoghourt*
*½-1 teaspoon hot pepper sauce*
*2 tablespoons (30 ml) soya sauce*
*2 small eggs, beaten with 1 tablespoon (15 ml) cornflour*
*1 medium green or red pepper, seeded and finely chopped*
*black pepper to taste*
*vegetable oil for shallow frying*
*tomato and lemon wedges to garnish*

Lightly grill the fish fillets on both sides (about 1 minute each side under a medium grill). Flake the fish into small pieces in a mixing bowl and stir in the coconut milk or yoghourt, hot pepper sauce, soya sauce, egg and cornflour and green or red pepper. Add black pepper to taste and thoroughly combine the mixture. Form into eight flattish fishcakes and shallow fry golden brown on both sides. Serve garnished with tomato and lemon wedges.

PREPARATION TIME 20 MINUTES

## Japanese One-Pot Fish Dishes

In Japanese, *nabe* means a pot or casserole, and *nabe-mono* are 'pot things'. The name is given to complete meals prepared in a single pan or casserole, a style of cooking which lends itself admirably to the lovely Japanese tradition of cooking at the table.

In this method of cooking, the diners are involved in the preparation of the meal, and the host and hostess can spend all their time with their guests. Cooking at the table also ensures that the food is eaten piping hot, and that it is cooked to just the degree chosen by each guest. Another attraction in Japan, where very few houses have central heating, is that the *hibachi* or table cooker gives off a warm glow, and what could be more pleasurable on a cold night than sitting around a charcoal burner eating hot food.

All the ingredients for a *nabe-mono* meal are prepared beforehand and attractively arranged on one or two large serving dishes. The guests sit around the table (a low table with cushions for sitting on is the best arrangement), and the food is cooked in a frying pan or casserole over a hotplate (electric, gas, paraffin or charcoal). Frying and boiling are the two principal cooking methods used for *nabe-mono*. The famous table meal *sukiyaki* (pronounced 'ski-yaki') is fried, and *mizutaki*, not well known in the West but very popular in Japan, is boiled. A recipe for a fish *sukiyaki* cooked at the table is given here as well as an adapted *mizutaki* dish which is served already cooked. Both recipes require a good fish stock (see p. 39).

# *Fish* Sukiyaki

SERVES 4

*Side dishes which normally accompany* sukiyaki *are miso soup, boiled rice, pickles and saké or tea.*

*1½ pints (900 ml) fish stock*
*1 tablespoon (15 ml) sugar*
*4 tablespoons (60 ml) saké or dry white wine*
*9 large Chinese cabbage leaves*
*8 oz (225 g) fresh spinach*
*2 in (5 cm) piece of fresh root ginger, peeled and grated*
*juice of 1 lemon*
*4 tablespoons (60 ml) soya sauce*
*2 tablespoons (30 ml) vegetable oil*
*4 × 8 oz (225 g) herring or mackerel fillets cut crosswise*
*6 spring onions, cut into 1½ in (3.75 cm) lengths*
*2 bamboo shoots, thinly sliced*
*12 oz (350 g) beancurd, cut into 1 in (2.5 cm) cubes*

Combine the fish stock, sugar and saké or wine, mix well and transfer the mixture to a jug.

Heat a pan of salted water to boiling and lightly parboil the Chinese cabbage leaves for ½-1 minutes. Lift them from the pot and rinse under cold water. Drain.

Collect the spinach leaves with stems all at one end. Return the salted water to the boil and, holding a small bunch of spinach by the stems, dip the leaves into the boiling water for ½-1 minute. Rinse under cold water and drain. Repeat for all the spinach.

Arrange three cabbage leaves overlapping on a *sudare* (bamboo mat) or thick moist cloth. Lay a third of the spinach leaves horizontally across the centre, alternating leaves and stems. Roll the cabbage leaves and spinach leaves up into tight bundles. Remove the *sudare* or cloth and cut the bundles into 1 in (2.5 cm) lengths. Repeat for all the cabbage leaves and spinach.

Mix the ginger, lemon juice and soya sauce and place in a small bowl.

Arrange the chopped cabbage rolls and remaining ingredients on one or two large serving dishes and lay them on the dining table with the sauce.

Set a hotplate on the table turned to medium and heat the oil in a heavy frying pan. Add the fish, lightly fry on both sides and then add half the cabbage roll pieces, half the spring onions and bamboo shoots and half the beancurd. Pour two thirds of the fish stock over the mixture and cook until the vegetables are tender. The guests may now help themselves to the cooked food, which is dipped into the ginger and lemon mixture before eating. Replenish the pan with the remaining vegetables, beancurd and fish stock as required.

PREPARATION TIME 45 MINUTES

▼ ▼ ▼ ▼ ▼ ▼ ▼ ▼ ▼ ▼ ▼ ▼ ▼ ▼ ▼ ▼ ▼ ▼ ▼ ▼ ▼ ▼ ▼ ▼ ▼ ▼ ▼ ▼ ▼ ▼ ▼

# *Fish* Mizutaki
### SERVES 4

*A one-pot fish dish served at the table directly from the casserole in which it is cooked.*
*Increase ingredient amounts accordingly for more diners.*

*4 dried shiitake (Japanese mushrooms) or 4 large fresh mushrooms, cleaned*
*4 × 8 oz (225 g) firm-fleshed white fish fillets such as halibut*
*or sea bream*
*1 medium onion, thinly sliced*
*1 canned bamboo shoot, cut into thin half-moon shapes*
*1 medium carrot, cut into 1 in (2.5 cm) lengths*
*1 clove garlic, crushed*
*1½ pints (900 ml) fish stock*
*1 in (2.5 cm) piece of fresh root ginger, peeled and grated*
*salt and black pepper*
*6 oz (175 g) beancurd, cut into 1 in (2.5 cm) cubes*
*2 spring onions, cut into 1 in (2.5 cm) pieces*
*4 tablespoons (60 ml) soya sauce*
*juice of 1 lemon*
*2 tablespoons (30 ml)* mirin *(Japanese sweet wine) or sherry*

Soak the shiitake in cold water for 20 minutes. Cut away the hard stems. Reserve the soaking water for use as part of the stock in the recipe. Ignore this stage if you are using fresh mushrooms.

Cut the fish fillets crosswise into 2 in (5 cm) wide pieces and put them into the casserole dish with the shiitake or fresh mushrooms, onion, bamboo shoot, carrot, garlic, stock, root ginger, and salt and black pepper to taste. Bring to the boil, reduce the heat, cover and simmer for 10 minutes. Now add the beancurd and spring onions, and simmer for a further 2 minutes.

Mix the soya sauce, lemon juice and *mirin* or sherry and divide the sauce among four small bowls.

Put the casserole directly onto the table, invite the guests to lift out with chopsticks pieces of cooked fish and vegetables and to dip them into the soya sauce and lemon mixture before eating. Finally, to finish off, ladle the stock into bowls for your guests to drink.

PREPARATION TIME 45 MINUTES

# CHICKEN

Chicken is a versatile food that lends itself to being cooked in many different ways with a variety of ingredients. Left-over cooked chicken is also always usable in sandwiches, salads, curries, stir-fry dishes and so on. It is economical, high in protein and low in fat, and the fat content may be further reduced by skinning the chicken or chicken pieces before cooking. Most of the fat in chicken is attached to the skin and it seeps into the flesh before cooking. However, the skin seals in moisture and flavour, so skinned chicken should be cooked in a sauce or, if the chicken is cooked whole, in a broth for basting.

In a demivegetarian diet chicken is sometimes used as the central ingredient of a main dish but also as a minor ingredient in a range of dishes such as soups, salads, casseroles and sauces. In this context it is convenient to have cooked chicken available in the refrigerator. Nowadays it is easy to buy precooked chicken pieces for this purpose, but it is simple, cheaper and perhaps more satisfying to cook it your-self. Recipes for simmered whole chicken and poached chicken pieces are given in the text.

Not so long ago chicken was one of those foods reserved for special occasions, and for some people Christmas was the only time they ate it. Nowadays it is a common and popular food, and the main reason for this is the advent of battery farming, which drastically reduced the price of chicken and increased its availability. This was a welcome development for some people, but for others it raised concerns about animal welfare and about the wisdom of eating meat from animals fed on growth-promoting hormones and antibiotics. Decisions about how to approach these problems are personal, but a middle path between ignoring the dilemma on the one hand or becoming a vegetarian on the other is to exclude red meat from our diets and to eat only a moderate amount of chicken. With the money saved by not buying meat, we can afford the more expensive free-range, maize- or grain-fed chickens. These birds taste better than their battery-reared cousins. The flesh is firmer, however, and they take a little longer to cook.

The recipes given here have been chosen to illustrate the versatility of chicken. Either whole chicken cut into portions or several pieces of a particular cut of chicken such as breast or thigh are suggested in the recipes, but they are normally interchangeable and may be substituted for each other. For very economical dishes chicken wings can be used.

To test if a whole chicken or chicken piece is cooked, stick a skewer into the centre of a thick fleshy part and withdraw it. There should be no trace of pinkness in the juice that then runs free.

## Simmered Chicken

SERVES 4–6

MAKES 1½ PINTS (800 ML) CHICKEN STOCK

*Chicken cooked in this way may be served hot with new potatoes, vegetables and a sauce (see Sauces, p. 89) for a simple but satisfying low-fat, nutritious meal, or kept in a refrigerator for later use in combination with wholegrains or vegetables or in sandwiches and salads. The recipe uses a whole chicken; if only small amounts of cooked chicken are required, two or three chicken joints can be used instead. Reserve the chicken stock which is produced and use it later in soups, stews, for cooking grains and so on.*

*3 lb (1.4 kg) roasting chicken, quartered*
*2 pints (1 litre) water*
*1 carrot, coarsely chopped*
*1 medium onion, quartered*
*2 bay leaves*
*4 whole peppercorns*
*4 whole allspice*
*salt to taste*

Put the chicken into a large, heavy pan and add all the other ingredients. Slowly bring to the boil and skim off any foam that forms. Once boiled, reduce the heat, cover and

*Top: Fennel and Grapefruit Salad (page 68) Bottom: Pear and Avocado with*
*Tahini Mayonnaise (page 55)*

*Preparation of Baked Fish (cod) with Fresh Shiitake Mushrooms (page 104)*

simmer for 1 hour or until the chicken is tender. Remove the chicken pieces and drain them into the pot. Set them aside until cool enough to handle. Strain off the chicken stock and discard the vegetables. Cut the chicken into pieces and either use immediately or store in the refrigerator until required.

PREPARATION TIME 1 HOUR 10 MINUTES

# Whole Chicken Simmered in Spiced Coconut Milk
### SERVES 6

*This is a very tasty and simple way of preparing whole chicken. The recipe includes quite a few ingredients, but they are easy to obtain, and the cooking method involves only two stages.*

*3–4 lb (1.4–1.8 kg) young chicken*
*2 tablespoons (30 ml) grated onion*
*1 red or green chilli pepper, seeded*
*3 cloves garlic*
*1 tablespoon (15 ml) peanut butter*
*2 teaspoons grated lemon rind*
*2 tablespoons (30 ml) fish sauce*
*1 teaspoon black pepper*
*1 teaspoon ground cumin*
*½ teaspoon ground ginger*
*16 fl oz (450 ml) tinned coconut milk or 3 oz (75 g) creamed coconut dissolved in 12 fl oz (350 ml) hot water*
*4 fl oz (100 ml) single cream*

*Garnish*
*dried red chillies, seeded, finely chopped (optional)*
*1 teaspoon ground coriander*

Put the chicken into a large saucepan. Put all the other ingredients except the coconut milk and coconut cream into a blender. Blend to a smooth paste. Add a little of the coconut milk to make the paste thinner and then stir the paste into the coconut milk. Pour this mixture over the chicken, bring to the boil, reduce the heat, cover the pan and simmer for 45-50 minutes or until the chicken is tender. During this time turn the chicken two or three times. Transfer the chicken to a warmed serving dish. Stir the single cream into the sauce left in the pan. Cook over a low heat, stirring, for 2-3 minutes. Pour the sauce over the chicken and garnish with chopped chillies and coriander.

PREPARATION TIME 1 HOUR

## Chicken with Lemon and Olives

SERVES 4–6

*Chicken, olives and spices with lemon juice provide an unusual and refreshing combination of flavours. Serve with couscous or rice.*

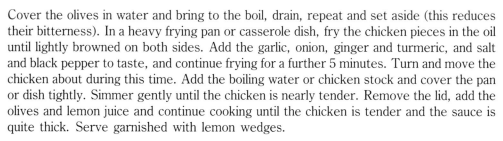

*8 oz (225 g) black or green olives or a mixture of the two*
*8 chicken thighs*
*4 fl oz (100 ml) oil*
*2 cloves garlic, crushed*
*1 small onion, finely sliced*
*1 teaspoon ground ginger*
*½ teaspoon turmeric*
*salt and black pepper*
*16 fl oz (450 ml) boiling water or chicken stock*
*juice of 2 lemons*
*lemon wedges for garnishing*

Cover the olives in water and bring to the boil, drain, repeat and set aside (this reduces their bitterness). In a heavy frying pan or casserole dish, fry the chicken pieces in the oil until lightly browned on both sides. Add the garlic, onion, ginger and turmeric, and salt and black pepper to taste, and continue frying for a further 5 minutes. Turn and move the chicken about during this time. Add the boiling water or chicken stock and cover the pan or dish tightly. Simmer gently until the chicken is nearly tender. Remove the lid, add the olives and lemon juice and continue cooking until the chicken is tender and the sauce is quite thick. Serve garnished with lemon wedges.

PREPARATION TIME 1 HOUR

## Fried Chicken with Garlic and Spinach

SERVES 4–6

*This dish is traditionally made with* melokhia, *a green leafy vegetable popular in Egypt, but spinach works just as well.*

*3 lb (1.5 kg) chicken jointed into eight pieces, or 8 chicken thighs*
*1 medium onion, halved*
*1 carrot*
*salt and black pepper*
*2 teaspoons coriander seeds, crushed*
*4 cloves garlic, crushed*
*2 teaspoons salt*
*4 oz (100 g) butter*
*1 lb (450 g) fresh spinach, washed, drained and chopped*

Put the chicken pieces, onion and carrot in a large pan, just cover with water, season to taste with salt and black pepper, and bring to the boil. Remove any froth as it forms. Cover, reduce the heat, and simmer until the chicken is tender (about 50 minutes). Remove the chicken, drain, and reserve the stock. Combine the coriander, garlic and salt and crush them into a paste. Clean the pan and in it melt the butter over a moderate heat. Stir in the paste and then add the chicken. Sauté the pieces, with turning, until they are coloured all over. Add the spinach and cook until it is wilted and tender. Adjust the seasoning and serve with rice. Serve the hot stock in separate bowls.

PREPARATION TIME 1 HOUR 10 MINUTES

# Moroccan Chicken with Chickpeas

SERVES 4–6

*In this dish the chicken is left whole during cooking and all the vital juices stay in the pot. Served with rice, it makes a delicious and nutritious meal.*

*3 lb (1.4 kg) roasting chicken*
*4 oz (100 g) butter or vegetable oil*
*3 medium onions, finely chopped*
*¾ teaspoon cayenne*
*1 teaspoon turmeric*
*4 cloves garlic, crushed*
*juice of 2 lemons*
*8 oz (225 g) chickpeas, soaked overnight and drained*
*water or stock*
*salt and black pepper*
*2 tablespoons (30 ml) finely chopped parsley*
*1 tablespoon (15 ml) raisins*

Clean the chicken inside and out with a damp cloth. Heat the butter or oil in a large, deep, flameproof casserole dish or saucepan (big enough to hold a whole chicken). Add a third of the onions and all the cayenne and turmeric and fry gently. Add the chicken and fry it, with turning, until it is nicely yellowed all over. Add the garlic, lemon juice, chickpeas and enough water or stock to cover. Season to taste with salt and black pepper. Bring to the boil, cover and simmer for 1 hour or until the chicken is tender. During the last half hour of cooking add the remaining onions, parsley and raisins. Towards the end of the cooking period, adjust the seasoning and, if the cooking liquid is too thin, leave the lid off the pan to reduce it. Serve with the chicken cut into pieces and the chickpea sauce poured over the top. If the chicken cooks before the chickpeas, remove it from the pan and set it in a warm oven until needed.

PREPARATION TIME 1 HOUR 15 MINUTES (EXCLUDING
12–24 HOURS SOAKING TIME FOR THE CHICKPEAS)

## Chinese Chicken and Walnuts
### SERVES 4

*This is an excellent recipe to use up leftover cooked chicken and, so long as you
remember to marinate the chicken ahead of time, it is quick to prepare. We normally
associate Chinese food with rice, but in many areas of China millet is a staple food. So,
for a change from rice try this dish with its undervalued (at least in Britain) grain.*

2 tablespoons (30 ml) sweet sherry
3 tablespoons (45 ml) soya sauce
1 oz (25 g) fresh root ginger, peeled and thinly sliced
1 lb (450 g) cooked chicken cut into thick strips 2 in (5 cm) long
3 tablespoons (45 ml) vegetable oil
1 clove garlic, crushed
8 oz (225 g) Chinese cabbage, shredded
1 green pepper, seeded and cut into thick strips 2 in (5 cm) long
2 sticks celery, cut into thin strips 2 in (5 cm) long
8 oz (225 g) chopped walnuts, lightly dry-roasted

Combine the sherry, soya sauce and ginger in a small bowl and add the chicken pieces.
Mix thoroughly with a spoon or your hands. Cover and leave to marinate for between 2
and 8 hours. Heat half the oil in a heavy frying pan or wok and add the garlic, Chinese
cabbage, green pepper, celery and walnuts and stir-fry over a medium heat for 5 minutes.
Set this mixture aside and add the remaining oil to the frying pan or wok. Drain the
chicken pieces and reserve the marinade. Stir-fry the chicken for 2-3 minutes, remove
the pan from the heat and add the marinade. Soya sauce burns easily so take care to avoid
this. Return the pan to the heat and add the vegetables and walnuts. Heat through and
serve.

PREPARATION TIME 25 MINUTES
(EXCLUDING 2–8 HOURS MARINATING TIME)

## Egyptian Grilled Chicken
### SERVES 4

*This recipe uses very few ingredients to produce chicken pieces as tasty as you have ever
had. For a barbecue version, see the variation at the end of the recipe.*

1 tender young chicken, quartered
salt and freshly ground black pepper
4 cloves garlic, crushed
6 tablespoons (90 ml) olive oil
juice of 2 medium-sized lemons

Season the chicken pieces with salt and black pepper. Combine the garlic, oil and lemon
juice in a shallow dish, add the chicken pieces and brush them all over with this mixture.

Leave to marinate for 1 hour.

To cook under a grill, preheat a moderate grill and oil the rack. Line the grill pan with foil. Drain the chicken pieces and place them skin side down on the rack. Set the pan under the grill so that the chicken pieces are at least 6 in (16 cm) away from the heat source. Grill, brushing occasionally with the marinade, until the upper side is nicely browned (about 20 minutes). Turn the chicken pieces over and repeat for the other side. Serve when the pieces are golden brown and crisp. Pour over them any cooking juices and remaining marinade.

PREPARATION TIME 1 HOUR 45 MINUTES
(INCLUDING 1 HOUR MARINATING TIME)

### Variation

To cook over charcoal, put the chicken pieces skin side up on a well-oiled rack and cook over a glowing charcoal fire. Brush often with the marinade and turn the pieces two or three times during cooking. Serve when brown and crisp but still moist on the inside.

# Deep-Fried Chicken in Broth

SERVES 4

*Deep-fried food has a universal appeal and in many parts of the world the most popular street foods are deep-fried. Unfortunately, if the frying oil is not fresh or hot enough, the food being fried absorbs the oil and becomes fatty. In this recipe pieces of chicken are deep-fried and then simmered in a ginger-flavoured broth. It is important to fry them crisp: the dish loses its appeal if they are soggy. This is a Japanese recipe and in Japanese cuisine chicken and ginger are common partners.*

*oil for deep-frying*
*2 lb (900 g) boned chicken cut into generous bite-sized pieces*
*cornflour for dusting*
*1½ pints (900 ml) chicken stock (use stock cubes if necessary)*
*2 tablespoons (30 ml) soya sauce*
*2 teaspoons honey*
*2 teaspoons finely grated root ginger*
*8 oz (225 g) Chinese cabbage, shredded*
*watercress to garnish*

Heat the oil in a deep frying pan to 350° F (175° C) or until a slight haze forms above it. Toss the chicken pieces in the cornflour to coat each individual piece lightly. Slip the chicken into the hot oil a few pieces at a time, separating and turning the individual pieces as they fry. Once they are golden brown, remove them and drain on absorbent paper. Repeat for all the chicken. Put the chicken, chicken stock and all the other ingredients except the watercress into a saucepan and bring to the boil. Reduce heat and simmer for 8-10 minutes. Serve in individual bowls, each garnished with a little watercress.

PREPARATION TIME 35 MINUTES

# *Chicken Stuffed with Mango and Ginger*

SERVES 6

*Chicken breasts are stuffed with fresh mango and ginger, cooked and served with a
spicy creamy sauce.*

*6 chicken breasts (supreme)*
*salt and freshly ground black pepper*
*1 ripe mango, sliced*
*1 teaspoon finely grated root ginger*
*juice of 1 lime*
*2 shallots, finely chopped*
*1 oz (25 g) butter*
*1 small carrot, chopped*
*1 clove garlic, crushed*
*1 teaspoon coriander seeds*
*3 cardamom pods*
*1 teaspoon cumin seeds*
*3 cloves*
*1 teaspoon ground cinnamon*
*8 oz (225 g) low-fat fromage frais*
*lime slices and fresh coriander leaves to garnish*

Preheat the oven to 375° F (190° C, gas mark 5). Slice the pockets of the chicken breasts
to enlarge the cavities for stuffing and season with salt and freshly ground black pepper.
Fill the cavities with slices of mango (reserve a little mango for garnishing) and half the
ginger. Sprinkle the lime juice over the chicken. Bake the chicken breasts in separate
packets of buttered tinfoil for 20 minutes.

Meanwhile sweat the shallots in the butter in a heavy-bottomed saucepan. Add the
carrot and the garlic and remove from the heat. In a grinder, crush the coriander seeds,
the seeds from the cardamom pods, the cumin seeds and the cloves. Add this spice
mixture, the cinnamon and the rest of the ginger to the pan. Stir well and then liquidize
the mixture with the *fromage frais*. Return to the pan to reheat gently. Add water if too
thick.

To serve, unwrap the cooked chicken breasts, spoon the sauce over the pieces and
garnish with the mango, slices of lime and fresh coriander leaves.

PREPARATION TIME 1 HOUR

# Chicken Satay with Spicy Peanut Sauce

## SERVES 6

*This recipe was given to me by a lady with Malaysian connections and is an excellent introduction to this type of cooking. The peanut sauce also goes very well with boiled new potatoes.*

*6 chicken breasts, boned and cut into 1 in (2.5 cm) cubes*

### Marinade

*4 oz (100 g) creamed coconut*
*2 teaspoons ground coriander seeds*
*2 teaspoons grated fresh root ginger*
*¼ teaspoon turmeric*
*½ teaspoon brown sugar*
*1½ oz (40 g) ground almonds*

### Sauce

*1 tablespoon (15 ml) chopped onion*
*2 tablespoons (30 ml) salted peanuts*
*1 teaspoon brown sugar*
*4 tablespoons (60 ml) peanut butter*
*3 teaspoons soya sauce*
*2 teaspoons lemon juice*
*½ teaspoon chilli powder*
*1 teaspoon tomato purée*

### Marinade

Break up the coconut and heat gently in a saucepan with enough water to form a thin cream consistency. Add the coriander, fresh ginger, turmeric, brown sugar and ground almonds. Take the pan off the heat and mix well. Add more water if the marinade has thickened. Divide the chicken cubes among six skewers (preferably bamboo). Coat with the coconut mixture and marinate for 2 hours.

### Sauce

Liquidize all the ingredients for the sauce, adding enough water for a thick soup-like consistency. Grill the chicken on the skewers and serve with rice, cucumber chunks, pieces of fresh pineapple and the peanut sauce.

PREPARATION TIME 40 MINUTES
MARINATING TIME 2 HOURS

▼▼▼▼▼▼▼▼▼▼▼▼▼▼▼▼▼▼▼▼▼▼▼▼▼▼▼▼▼▼▼▼▼▼▼▼

## Steamed Chicken and Brown Rice
### SERVES 4

*In this recipe the chicken and the vegetables are painted with a soya sauce paste and then steamed over the rice while it is cooking. Do not restrict yourself to the vegetables suggested here, but experiment with other combinations. No cooking oil or fat is used in this recipe and it is a low-fat protein and rice combination. Serve it with a spicy tahini and yoghourt sauce (see p. 89).*

1 tablespoon (15 ml) cornflour
1 tablespoon (15 ml) water
3 tablespoons (45 ml) soya sauce
1 tender young chicken, skinned and jointed, or 4 smallish chicken breasts, skinned
1 large green pepper, seeded and cut into thick strips
2 sticks of celery, cut into 2 in (5 cm) pieces
2 medium-sized courgettes, halved
8 oz (225 g) brown rice, washed and drained
1½ pints (900 ml) water or chicken stock
salt

Make a paste of the cornflour, water and soya sauce and lightly brush it over the chicken pieces and vegetables. Set them aside. Put the rice and water or stock in a large, heavy saucepan or casserole dish and bring quickly to the boil, reduce the heat, and simmer, covered, until the rice is just firm enough to support the chicken and vegetables resting on top (about 15 minutes). At this point salt the rice to taste. Place the chicken and vegetables on the rice, reduce the heat to very low, and cover the pan. Cook until the rice and chicken are tender (about another 35-40 minutes).

PREPARATION TIME 1 HOUR 10 MINUTES

▼▼▼▼▼▼▼▼▼▼▼▼▼▼▼▼▼▼▼▼▼▼▼▼▼▼▼▼▼▼▼▼▼▼▼

## Marinated Chicken Donburi
### SERVES 4

*Donburi means 'big bowl' in Japanese and donburi dishes are large bowls of rice served with vegetables and egg or skewered chicken or meat. In this dish cubes of lean chicken are marinated in a sweet soya sauce, grilled and served with a sauce over rice. Serve with stir-fried vegetables or a salad.*

4 tablespoons (60 ml) soya sauce
2 teaspoons sugar
2 cloves garlic, crushed
1 lb (450 g) chicken breasts, skinned and boned and cut into 1 in (2.5 cm) cubes
1 lb (450 g) long-grain white rice, washed and drained
2 tablespoons (30 ml) sweet sherry or mirin (Japanese sweet wine)
4 fl oz (100 ml) chicken stock (use a stock cube if necessary)

Combine 3 tablespoons (45 ml) of the soya sauce with the sugar and garlic in a bowl big enough to hold the chicken pieces, mix them well together and add the chicken cubes. Stir the chicken around in the marinade to coat each piece. Set aside for 1 or more hours.

Twenty minutes before the dish is to be served put the rice on to cook. Then combine the sherry, or *mirin*, the remaining soya sauce and the stock in a small pan. Set it aside. Drain the chicken and reserve any marinade.

Thread the chicken cubes onto four small bamboo or metal skewers (if you use bamboo, wrap the ends in foil to stop them burning). Line a grill pan with foil and oil the rack. Preheat the grill to medium and grill the skewered chicken for several minutes, turning now and again, until they are nicely browned and tender. Occasionally baste with marinade. Meanwhile bring the sherry sauce to the boil. Drain the rice, arrange it in a shallow dish and place the skewers of chicken on top. Pour the sauce over the top and serve.

PREPARATION TIME 1 HOUR 10 MINUTES
(INCLUDING 1 HOUR MARINATING TIME)

## Chicken in Lemon Sauce with Spring Onions
SERVES 4

*This is a deliciously light summer dish, probably of Chinese origin.*

2 lemons
4 spring onions, finely chopped
½ teaspoon white sugar
1 small clove garlic, crushed
5 fl oz (150 ml) water
½ teaspoon salt
¾ teaspoon cornflour
4 chicken breasts, boned and slightly chilled
1 egg beaten with 2 teaspoons dry sherry
salt and freshly ground black pepper
vegetable oil

Cut four half slices from one of the lemons for a garnish and reserve for later use. Remove the peel and pith from the rest of this lemon and from the second one. Cut the flesh into half slices and place them in a large pan with the spring onions, sugar, garlic, water and salt. Add the cornflour and gently heat and stir until the sauce has lightly thickened.

Cut the chilled chicken into very thin slices with a sharp knife. Season the beaten egg mixture with salt and freshly ground black pepper, dip the slices of chicken into the mixture and fry them very quickly in a hot frying pan sparingly brushed with vegetable oil. Place them on a serving dish, pour the hot lemon sauce over the top and garnish with the reserved lemon slices. Serve with rice.

PREPARATION TIME 30 MINUTES

# White Curried Chicken

## SERVES 4–6

*This Indonesian mild curry dish is cooked in coconut milk which gives it a pale colour.
It is ideal for people who do not like hot curries. For individuals who wish to pep it up,
serve a small side dish of chilli sauce. For a fruity version, see the variation at the end
of the recipe.*

*1 teaspoon ground coriander*
*1 teaspoon ground cumin*
*¼ teaspoon ground cloves*
*½ teaspoon ground turmeric*
*¼ teaspoon chilli powder*
*3 tablespoons (45 ml) vegetable oil*
*2 medium onions, finely sliced*
*4 cloves garlic, crushed*
*1 teaspoon finely chopped root ginger*
*1 medium roasting or frying chicken cut into serving pieces or 8 chicken pieces*
*1 teaspoon grated lemon rind or 1 stalk lemon grass*
*2 bay leaves or daun salem leaves*
*16 fl oz (450 ml) canned coconut milk or 4 oz (100 g) creamed coconut
dissolved in 16 fl oz (450 ml) hot water*
*1 tablespoon (15 ml) lemon juice*

Combine the coriander, cumin, cloves, turmeric and chilli powder in a bowl and stir the
mixture to a paste with a little of the oil. Heat the remaining oil in a heavy frying pan or
wok and fry the onion, garlic and ginger until the onion is softened. Add the spice paste
and chicken pieces and stir them together over the heat until the chicken pieces are
coloured by the spices. Add the lemon rind or lemon grass, bay leaves or daun salem
leaves, and coconut milk and bring the mixture to a gentle boil. Reduce the heat and
simmer, uncovered, over a low heat for 50 minutes or until the chicken is tender and the
sauce is thick. Stir in the lemon juice and add salt to taste.

PREPARATION TIME 1 HOUR 10 MINUTES

## Variation
When the chicken is half cooked add 8 oz (225 g) fresh or tinned pineapple pieces to the
pan. Towards the end of the cooking period add two or three sliced bananas. Heat
through before serving.

# Chicken and Apricot Tagine

### SERVES 4

*This Moroccan stew combines fruit and chicken to give a delicious blend of flavours.*
*The apricots may be replaced by prunes, soaked overnight, or by fresh dates, apple slices*
*or pear slices. The dish is traditionally served hot with cayenne and I have left the*
*quantity to be added to your own judgement.*
*For a low-fat version of this recipe, see below.*

*2 oz (50 g) butter*
*8 chicken thighs or drumsticks or 4 chicken breasts cut in half*
*2 cloves garlic, crushed*
*½ teaspoon turmeric or saffron*
*½ teaspoon ground coriander*
*½ teaspoon ground cumin*
*¼ teaspon ground ginger*
*salt, black pepper and cayenne*
*2 medium onions, finely sliced*
*8 oz (225 g) dried whole apricots, soaked overnight*
*juice of 1 lemon*

Melt the butter in a heavy saucepan. Add the chicken pieces and sauté them on both sides until nicely browned. Stir in the garlic and spices, and season to taste with salt, black pepper and cayenne. Cook for a further 5 minutes and add half the onion, the water the apricots were soaked in (but not the apricots) and enough extra water just to cover the chicken. Bring to the boil, reduce the heat, cover, and simmer for 30 minutes or until the chicken is tender. After 20 minutes of this time add the remaining onion. Add more water as needed, but at the end of the cooking period the sauce should be thick. When the chicken is tender, add the apricots and continue cooking until the fruit is soft but not disintegrating. Adjust the seasoning if necessary and serve with rice or couscous (see p. 138) and bread.

### PREPARATION TIME 1 HOUR

### Variation

Sometimes the chicken or other meat for a tagine is not fried and the stewing time is increased. This method seems to give a richer flavour to the sauce and is worth trying. Follow the recipe as above but do not fry the chicken (the butter is thus not needed) and simmer the tagine very gently for 1¼ hours. Add the apricots or other fruit after 1 hour.

## Honey-Roasted Chicken
### SERVES 4–6

*This Middle Eastern roasting method uses little fat and produces a sweet, golden-brown chicken. A garnishing of chopped ginger and almonds completes the picture.*

*1 lemon*
*3-4 lb (1.4-1.8 kg) roasting chicken, cleaned and wiped dry*
*salt*
*2 oz (50 g) butter*
*4 tablespoons (60 ml) clear honey*

### Garnish
*preserved ginger, chopped*
*roasted almonds, chopped*

Preheat the oven to 450° F (230° C, gas mark 8). Cut the lemon in two and with half rub the chicken inside and out. Sprinkle the chicken inside and out with salt. Melt the butter and whisk it into the honey together with the juice of the remaining half lemon. Brush the chicken inside and out with this mixture. Place the chicken in an oiled roasting pan and place in the preheated oven. Reduce the heat after 10 minutes to 350° F (175° C, gas mark 4) and cook for about 20 minutes per lb (450 g) of bird plus 20 minutes. Baste occasionally during cooking.

Serve the chicken jointed and garnished with preserved ginger and chopped almonds. If you wish to reduce the cooking time, joint the chicken before roasting.

PREPARATION TIME APPROXIMATELY 1½ HOURS

## Traditional Japanese Chicken Teriyaki
### SERVES 4

*In Japanese cooking, fish, chicken or meat cooked teriyaki style is fried or grilled until nearly tender and then finished off in a sweet soya-sauce-based glaze.*

*2 chicken legs (thigh and drumstick) or breasts, boned*
*2 teaspoons vegetable oil*
*4 fl oz (100 ml) dry white wine or saké*
*4 fl oz (100 ml) medium sweet sherry or mirin*
*2 fl oz (50 ml) soya sauce*
*1 tablespoon (15 ml) sugar*
*2 cloves garlic, crushed*
*lemon wedges and/or cucumber strips and/or stir-fried green pepper strips*

Prick the skin of the chicken with a fork. Heat the oil in a frying pan and fry the chicken pieces skin side down until browned. Turn the chicken over, cover the pan and fry for 10 minutes over a low heat. Meanwhile combine the remaining ingredients in a small pan, bring to the boil, and remove from the heat.

Remove the chicken pieces from the frying pan and pour in the *teriyaki* sauce. Stir and return to the boil. Return the chicken to the pan and, over a high heat, reduce the *teriyaki* sauce, turning the chicken continuously. After a few minutes the chicken will be thickly coated and most of the sauce used up. Remove the chicken from the pan and slice it, skin side up, into ¾ in (2 cm) thick pieces. Arrange the chicken slices on four white plates. Garnish and serve.

PREPARATION TIME 25 MINUTES

## Lemon and Ginger Fried Chicken and Mushrooms
### SERVES 4

*This simple but very tasty dish is typical of Southeast Asian cooking. I have substituted lemon rind and lemon juice for lemon grass and tamarind water but the dish retains the myriad flavours so enjoyable in Thai and Indonesian food.*

*8 dried Chinese mushrooms or 8 oz (225 g) fresh mushrooms*
*3 tablespoons (45 ml) vegetable oil*
*2 teaspoons finely chopped root ginger*
*4 cloves garlic, crushed*
*1 red chilli pepper, seeded and finely chopped (optional)*
*3 lb (1.4. kg) roasting chicken divided into serving pieces or 8 chicken thighs or 4 chicken breasts cut in half*
*2 tablespoons (30 ml) lemon juice*
*2 teaspoons grated lemon rind*
*6 fl oz (175 ml) chicken stock or water*
*2 tablespoons (30 ml) fish sauce or soya sauce*
*freshly ground black pepper*
*finely chopped coriander leaves to garnish*

Soak the Chinese mushrooms in hot water for 30 minutes. Drain, remove and discard the stems, and slice the caps. Alternatively chop the fresh mushrooms. Heat the oil in a wok or large saucepan and stir-fry the ginger, garlic and chilli pepper (if used) until the garlic is just golden. Add the chicken pieces and fry them, stirring regularly, over a medium heat until nicely browned all over. Add the mushrooms, lemon juice, lemon rind, stock or water, fish sauce or soya sauce and black pepper to taste. Mix well, bring to the boil, cover, and cook over a moderate heat, stirring occasionally, for 25 minutes or until the chicken is tender. Serve garnished with coriander leaves.

PREPARATION TIME 1 HOUR (INCLUDING 30 MINUTES TO SOAK
DRIED MUSHROOMS)

# Fried Chicken Balinese Style

### SERVES 4–6

*In this recipe the chicken is fried in a spicy paste until half cooked, then coconut milk or*
*cow's milk is added and the chicken is simmered until tender. The result is a very*
*tender, spicy chicken dish with a slightly crisp texture.*

*2 tablespoons (30 ml) vegetable oil*
*3 lb (1.4 kg) roasting chicken, cut into serving pieces, or 8 chicken thighs or 4*
*chicken breasts cut in half*
*1 medium onion, chopped*
*½–1 fresh or dried chilli pepper, seeded and chopped (optional)*
*2 cloves garlic, crushed*
*1 teaspoon finely grated root ginger*
*1 oz (25 g) roasted almonds*
*1 tablespoon (15 ml) soya sauce*
*½ teaspoon ground cumin*
*1 teaspoon ground coriander*
*½ teaspoon ground turmeric*
*8 fl oz (225 ml) tinned coconut milk or 8 fl oz (225 ml) cow's milk*
*2 teaspoons cider vinegar*
*2 teaspoons dark brown sugar*
*salt*
*freshly chopped coriander leaves to garnish (optional)*

Heat the oil in a wok or frying pan and fry the chicken pieces over a moderate heat until browned and nearly cooked in the middle (about 3 minutes on each side). Remove the chicken pieces and set them aside. Put the onion, chilli (if used), garlic, ginger, almonds and soya sauce into a liquidizer and blend them into a smooth paste. Drain the frying oil from the wok or pan leaving only 2-3 tablespoons (30-45 ml). Stir in the onion paste, cumin, coriander, and turmeric and stir-fry the mixture for 2 minutes. Reduce the heat, add the coconut milk or cow's milk, vinegar and sugar and stir the mixture well. Add salt to taste. Add the chicken pieces and simmer, uncovered, until the chicken is tender and the sauce is thick (about 20-30 minutes). Do not boil the coconut liquor or it may curdle. Garnish with coriander leaves if available.

PREPARATION TIME 45 MINUTES

# Hot Spiced Chicken with Lemon Juice

SERVES 4–6

*In this North African dish the chicken is rubbed with spicy garlic mixture and then fried
before being casseroled in water, spices and tomato purée. Finally the dish is given its
distinctive taste by the addition of lemon juice. Serve with rice and/or pitta bread, or see
the variation below.*

3 lb (1.4 kg) roasting chicken
1 tablespoon (15 ml) salt
3 cloves garlic, crushed
½ teaspoon cayenne pepper
1 teaspoon turmeric
3 tablespoons (45 ml) olive oil or melted butter
2 medium onions, finely chopped
4 cloves
2 teapoons cumin seeds
1 teaspoon coriander seeds
2 tablespoons (30 ml) tomato purée
6 fl oz (175 ml) water
juice of 2 lemons

Cut the chicken into serving pieces and wipe them dry. Combine the salt, garlic, cayenne
and turmeric, and rub the mixture into the skin side of the chicken pieces. Leave for 15
minutes. Heat the oil or melted butter in a large, heavy frying pan and brown the chicken
on both sides. Remove the pieces to a plate and in the same oil lightly fry the chopped
onions until just soft. Stir in the cloves, cumin and coriander seeds and continue frying.
After a few minutes stir in the tomato purée and return the chicken pieces to the pan.
Add the water, cover the pan tightly, and simmer *very* gently for 1 hour or until the
chicken is tender. After 45 minutes' cooking add the lemon juice and adjust the seasoning
to taste.

PREPARATION TIME 1 HOUR 45 MINUTES

## Variation

This dish is excellent cooked with rice, and the procedure requires little adjustment to
the recipe. Wash and drain 1½ cups long-grain rice. Add it to the chicken after 35-40
minutes' cooking and also pour in 1½ cups boiling water. Cover the pan tightly and
simmer gently until rice and chicken are both tender. Lightly stir once during cooking.
Transfer the contents of the pan to one large serving dish, arranging the chicken pieces
on top of the rice, and serve.

# Yoghourt-Marinated Chicken Curry

SERVES 4

*In this Indian dish chicken pieces are marinated in a spicy yoghourt mixture before cooking. This tenderizes and flavours the chicken. Serve with white, brown or saffron rice (see p. 137), chutney and a crisp green salad.*

*2 cloves garlic, crushed*
*1 teaspoon crushed cumin seeds*
*¼ teaspoon chilli powder or sauce*
*½ teaspoon crushed mustard seeds*
*1 teaspoon turmeric powder*
*1 in (2.5 cm) root ginger, grated*
*1 tablespoon (15 ml) vegetable oil*
*8 fl oz (225 ml) natural yoghourt*
*8 chicken thighs, skinned, or 4 chicken breasts, skinned and cut in half*
*3 oz (75 g) ghee or butter*
*2 medium onions, chopped*
*16 fl oz (450 ml) water*
*salt to taste*
*2 cardamom pods to garnish*

Stir the garlic, cumin, chilli, mustard seeds, turmeric powder, ginger and oil into the yoghourt and mix well together. Put the chicken pieces (if using breasts, place skinned sides up) in a shallow dish and brush or pour the yoghourt marinade over them. Set aside to marinate for 1-3 hours.

Heat the ghee or butter in a large heavy saucepan, add the onions and sauté until golden. Add the chicken and yoghourt marinade, stir gently, cover the pan and very gently simmer for 5 minutes. Add the water and salt to taste. Carefully stir again. Bring to a shallow boil. Cover, reduce the heat, and simmer for 30 minutes or until the chicken is tender. Peel the cardamom pods, crush the seeds and serve the curry garnished with them.

PREPARATION TIME 45 MINUTES (PLUS 1–3 HOURS MARINATING TIME)

# GRAINS AND PASTA

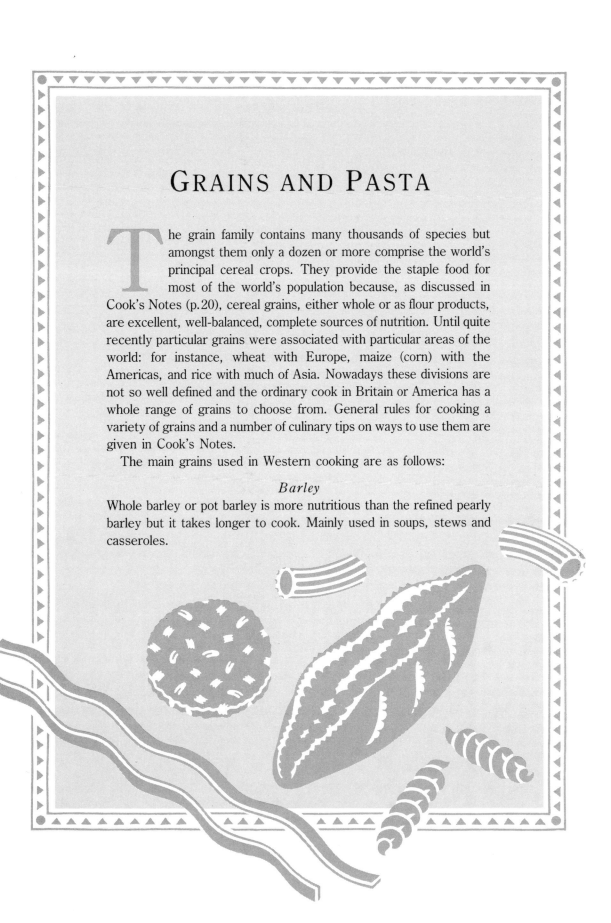

The grain family contains many thousands of species but amongst them only a dozen or more comprise the world's principal cereal crops. They provide the staple food for most of the world's population because, as discussed in Cook's Notes (p.20), cereal grains, either whole or as flour products, are excellent, well-balanced, complete sources of nutrition. Until quite recently particular grains were associated with particular areas of the world: for instance, wheat with Europe, maize (corn) with the Americas, and rice with much of Asia. Nowadays these divisions are not so well defined and the ordinary cook in Britain or America has a whole range of grains to choose from. General rules for cooking a variety of grains and a number of culinary tips on ways to use them are given in Cook's Notes.

The main grains used in Western cooking are as follows:

### Barley

Whole barley or pot barley is more nutritious than the refined pearly barley but it takes longer to cook. Mainly used in soups, stews and casseroles.

### Buckwheat

Not strictly a grain but the seed of a herbaceous plant, buckwheat is popular in Russia and other Eastern European countries. The grain, or kasha as it is also called, loses some of its flavour if it is not dry-roasted before cooking. Buy preroasted buckwheat or dry-roast the plain variety before boiling it (see p.20). Kasha has an interesting nutty flavour. It is good served on its own or as an ingredient in savoury dishes and patties. Crushed buckwheat and buckwheat flour are used in pancake and muffin batters.

### Corn (maize)

Five varieties of corn are grown commercially, but only two, corn on the cob and dent corn, from which cornmeal is ground, are of interest to the cook. Whole maize or cornmeal retains all the goodness of the corn. Stoneground is the best if you can obtain it. Polenta is the Italian name for yellow maize or cornmeal. It is a staple food in parts of northern Italy, where boiled polenta, cooled and then fried, sometimes takes the place of bread. Cornflour is not as nutritious as whole maize flour, but is excellent for thickening soups and sauces.

### Millet

In the West, millet is generally demoted to an animal food, but why this is so is a mystery. Nutritionally millet compares well with other cereals, and the cooked grains and flours are delicious. It contains vitamins of the B complex, important minerals, especially iron, and 9 per cent by weight of protein. Millet grain is usually hulled since the outer part is too hard to cook. Fortunately this does not involve a large nutrient loss and millet grain is almost as nutritious as whole millet flour which includes the milled hull or bran section of the grain. Many peoples with long life expectancy, including the famous Hunzas of the Himalayas, cultivate millet as a staple crop.

### Oats

Oats are a rich source of nutrients. They are used mostly in breakfast cereals but can also be added to soups, stews and other savoury dishes. Oatmeal flour is used in bread and cake making. Oats are traditionally the main ingredient of muesli, which was formulated by the Swiss nutritionist Dr Bircher-Benner over seventy years ago. The recipe was devised to provide a meal that supplied good amounts of protein, vitamins, minerals and roughage without overloading the body with too much rich food. Muesli is considered by most nutritionists to be an excellent food combination.

### Rice

Rice is an excellent food for the cook. It is versatile and adaptable, and once you have learned to judge how to cook it well you can make a good plain boiled rice and combination rice dishes without fail. Before it is cooked, rice should be washed. American- or European-packed rice only needs a light rinse, but loose rice or Asian-packed rice should be rinsed in a colander until the water stops running milky. If the starch is washed away before cooking it is not necessary to do so again afterwards. If cooked rice needs draining because it has been cooked in too much water, it will lose nutrients and flavour.

Brown rice is more nutritious than white; if you enjoy its flavour and also have time to cook it, you will benefit from including it in your diet. If, as some people do, you prefer white rice, make sure the rest of your diet is well mixed and that it includes fruit and vegetables for the fibre.

Long-grain rice (often called patna rice since it was thought to have originated from Patna in India) remains in separate grains and becomes light and fluffy when cooked. It is excellent for serving on its own, as well as in pilavs, risottos, paellas, and so on. Short-grain rices are soft when cooked and the grains stick gently to one another. For savoury dishes, except in Japan and parts of China, most people prefer long-grain rice. Short-grain rice is also used for desserts, just as we use pudding rice (a short-grain variety) to make rice pudding.

Wild rice is a cereal grain native to North America, China and Japan. It is in the same broad family as the rice plant but it has never been domestically cultivated. Raw wild rice is brown, but it acquires a faint purplish colour when cooked. It has a delicate, nutty flavour.

### Wheat and wheat products

There are numerous ways of cooking wheat and wheat flour products. The variety of cooking methods has, of course, resulted from regional differences, types of wheat available, cultural traditions, the influence of technology and, not least, human inventiveness.

### Bulgar wheat

This is parboiled, cracked wheat. Although relatively unknown in the West, bulgar wheat is the staple food of some countries of the Middle East, where it is served with rice and also used as the basis for a variety of cold salads. Bulgar has all the nutritional qualities of wholewheat grain. It has a distinctive taste and is easy to cook.

### Semolina (couscous and pasta)

Semolina is produced from the starchy endosperm of the wheat grain. It is milled in various grades to give fine, medium or coarse semolina. Fine semolina is used in puddings and pasta production, while coarse semolina is used to make couscous.

Couscous is probably the most common and most widely known North African Arab dish. The grains are steamed over a rich sauce or stew and then served in a mountainous heap with the sauce poured over the top. Couscous is never cooked in the sauce. Traditionally, the stew is made with mutton or chicken, though a vegetable variation is just as tasty (see p.81).

Pasta Italian style is made from a dough of wheat flour, eggs and water. The dough is rolled out and cut into any of a huge variety of shapes, then dried, before being cooked in water. The best pasta is made from hard-grained wheats, particularly durum wheat.

Wholemeal pasta is more nutritious and is higher in protein than normal white-flour pasta.

When cooking pasta the important rule is to use a large pot and plenty of water. Generally 1 lb (450 g) pasta needs 6 pints (3 litres) water. For salt, 1½ tablespoons (22.5 ml) per-lb (450 g) pasta is an average amount, added after the water has boiled and before the pasta is put in. To prevent the pasta sticking to itself during cooking, a little butter or oil is added to the water. The water is brought to a rolling boil, salted, about 2 tablespoons (30 ml) oil are added and the pasta is then carefully fed into the pot and boiled, uncovered, until it is soft on the outside but with a slight resistance at the centre (*al dente*). Cooking times vary depending on the type of pasta and whether it is bought or homemade. As soon as the pasta is cooked, drain it in a colander and serve with a sauce or grated cheese or on its own with olive oil and freshly ground black pepper.

# Chickpea and Brown Rice Pilav

SERVES 4

*This is a wholesome and tasty one-dish meal.*

*4 oz (100 g) chickpeas soaked overnight and drained,*
*or 8 oz (25 g) tinned chickpeas*
*2 oz (50 g) butter or vegetable oil*
*1 medium onion, finely sliced*
*1 clove garlic, crushed*
*1 teaspoon cumin seeds, crushed*
*1 teaspoon coriander seeds, crushed*
*1 in (2.5 cm) cinnamon stick*
*1 teaspoon turmeric*
*½ teaspoon chilli powder*
*½ teaspoon ground ginger*
*1 medium carrot, cut into matchsticks*
*1 medium red or green pepper, seeded and diced*
*1 large stick celery, finely chopped*
*10 fl oz (300 ml) long-grain brown rice (measure by volume), washed and*
*drained*
*1 pint (550 ml) boiling water*
*salt and black pepper*
*2 oz (50 g) dry-roasted almonds*

Cover the chickpeas with water in a pan, bring to the boil, reduce the heat, cover, and set to simmer for 1 hour. Meanwhile heat the butter or oil in a heavy-bottomed saucepan and sauté the onion and garlic until softened. Add the cumin, coriander, cinnamon, turmeric, chilli powder and ginger. Stir well and sauté for a further 2 minutes. Add the carrot, red or green pepper and celery. Stir and cook for 5 minutes. Stir in the rice and then add the boiling water. Season to taste with salt and black pepper. Cover the pan and gently simmer for 45 minutes. Once the chickpeas are tender, drain them and stir them into the cooking rice. By the end of the cooking period the rice should be tender but still firm and the contents of the pan should be moist but not sloppy. Tip the pilav into a serving dish, remove the cinnamon stick and garnish with roasted almonds.

PREPARATION TIME 1½ HOURS
SOAKING TIME 12 HOURS (OR USE TINNED CHICKPEAS)

### Variations

Other vegetables may be substituted or added to this dish, such as green beans, aubergines, fresh or frozen green peas or potatoes. To make the pilav hotter, add ½–1 finely chopped red chilli with the other spices. Curry powder can also be used. Add up to 1 teaspoon with the other spices.

*Note*: If you are cooking chickpeas for a dish which does not require a large amount, cook more than you need and use the leftovers in other ways, for example, in salads, stuffings, dips or soups. Cooking small amounts of pulses is uneconomical. The alternative is to have tinned chickpeas available for such occasions. Both tinned red beans and chickpeas are usually good.

## Leek and Kasha Pie

#### SERVE 4

*Kasha is roasted buckwheat (see p.20 for roasting method). It has an interesting nutty flavour and makes a pleasant change from regular grains. This dish also includes bean curd in the ingredients, illustrating the versatility of this recent addition to the Western cook's repertoire.*

4 oz (100 g) raw kasha
1 medium onion, chopped
4 large leeks, trimmed, washed and sliced
2 teaspoons chopped fresh thyme or ½ teaspoon dried thyme
2 teaspoons chopped fresh marjoram or ½ teaspoon dried marjoram
1 bay leaf
2 tablespoons (30 ml) vegetable oil
1 clove garlic
4 oz (100 g) beancurd, drained
¼ pint (150 ml) béchamel sauce (see p.90)
2 tablespoons (30 ml) soya sauce
2 oz (50 g) cheese, grated
1 oz (25 g) wholemeal breadcrumbs

Cook the kasha in twice its own volume of water for 20 minutes or until tender. Meanwhile preheat the oven to 400° F (200° C, gas mark 6). In a covered saucepan sauté the onion, leeks, thyme, marjoram and the bay leaf in the oil for 10 minutes. Line the base of a greased casserole dish with the mixture and put the cooked kasha on top. Put the garlic, beancurd, béchamel sauce and soya sauce in a liquidizer and blend for 2 minutes. Pour this mixture over the kasha and top with the grated cheese and breadcrumbs mixed together. Bake for 40 minutes in the hot oven.

PREPARATION TIME 1 HOUR 15 MINUTES

## Barley and Lentil Patties

SERVES 6

*7 oz (225 g) whole barley*
*4 oz (100 g) red lentils*
*5 oz (150 g) grated Cheddar cheese*
*1 small egg, beaten*
*2 tablespoons (30 ml) tomato purée*
*½ teaspoon salt*
*½ teaspoon freshly ground black pepper*
*1½ oz (40 g) wholemeal flour*
*1 tablespoon (15 ml) finely chopped parsley*
*sunflower seed oil for shallow frying*

Cook the barley in plenty of water until tender (allow up to 45 minutes for this). Cook the lentils separately in at least twice their volume of water. Drain both the barley and lentils and combine them with all the other ingredients except the oil. Mix well and form into patties approximately ½ in (1.25 cm) thick. Shallow-fry until golden brown in hot sunflower seed oil. Serve hot either with the cold garlic and yoghourt sauce given with the falafel on p.149 or with a good homemade hot tomato sauce (see p.90).

PREPARATION T'ME 1 HOUR

## Bulgar Wheat with Cheese and Aubergines

SERVES 4

*A simple dish, easy to prepare and surprisingly tasty and combining*
*three food groups in a nutritious balance.*

*1 medium aubergine, cut into ¾ in (2 cm) cubes, salted and pressed for*
*30 minutes, rinsed and drained*
*2 tablespoons (30 ml) olive oil*
*8 oz (225 g) bulgar wheat*
*10 fl oz (300 ml) water*
*4 oz (100 g) mozzarella or Cheddar cheese, cut into ¾ in (2 cm) cubes*
*salt and black pepper*

Dry the aubergine cubes on kitchen paper or a tea towel. Heat the oil in a frying pan or wok and gently fry the aubergines until just tender. Remove them from the pan with a slotted spoon and set aside. Add the bulgar wheat to the pan and stir over a low heat for a few minutes to coat it lightly with the oil left in the pan. Add the water slowly so that it does not spit too much, stir well and simmer until the bulgar is tender (about 7–8 minutes). Add the aubergine cubes, heat through and then stir in the cheese and salt and pepper to taste. Remove from the heat, set aside, covered, for 5 minutes and then serve.

PREPARATION TIME 50 MINUTES
(INCLUDING 30 MINUTES TO SALT THE AUBERGINES)

# Thai Fried Rice

SERVES 4

*Fried rice is a convenient way of using up cold leftover cooked rice, which fries much better than freshly cooked rice. Make sure, however, that the cooked rice smells fresh and is safe to use. Fried rice is a dish to improvise with and the method given here is only one of many. In the Thai manner, it is hot and also flavoured with coriander leaves. For an exotic use of fried rice, see Rice-Stuffed Pineapple below.*

*3 tablespoons (45 ml) vegetable oil*
*2 cloves garlic, finely chopped*
*1 medium onion, finely chopped*
*1 red or green chilli pepper, seeded and chopped*
*1 in (2.5 cm) root ginger, peeled and cut into fine slivers (optional)*
*2 tablespoons (30 ml) soya sauce*
*1 lb (450 g) cooked rice*
*2 tablespoons (30 ml) tomato purée*

## Garnish
*1 small or 1/2 medium cucumber, sliced*
*2 tablespoons (30 ml) chopped coriander leaves*

Heat the oil in a wok or large saucepan. Add the garlic and onion and fry until the onion is softened. Add the chilli pepper and ginger (if used) and stir-fry for 2 minutes. Add the soya sauce, stir well and then add the rice and tomato purée. Stir-fry until the rice is well heated through. Transfer to a serving dish. Surround the edge of the plate with cucumber slices and garnish the rice with coriander leaves. Serve immediately.

PREPARATION TIME 20 MINUTES

# Rice-Stuffed Pineapple

SERVES 4–6

*Cut the top off a large pineapple about a quarter of the way down. Scoop out all the flesh. Cut it into cubes and add 8 oz (225 g) with the chilli pepper and ginger to the Thai Fried Rice above. Preheat the oven to 350° F (180° C, gas mark 4). Stuff the hollowed-out pineapple with the pineapple fried rice, put the top back on and bake it for 15 minutes.*

## Cashew and Almond Pilav

SERVES 4

*In this Indian recipe some of the spices are left whole. They are not removed
after cooking, but neither are they eaten.*

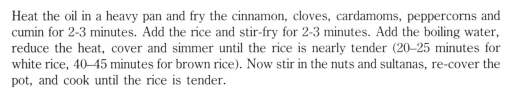

3 tablespoons (45 ml) butter or vegetable oil
1 in (2.5 cm) cinnamon stick
3 cloves
3 cardamom pod seeds
6 peppercorns
½ teaspoon cumin seeds
12 oz (350 g) rice (brown or white)
1½ pints (900 ml) boiling water
2 oz (50 g) blanched almonds
2 oz (50 g) lightly roasted cashews
2 oz (50 g) sultanas

Heat the oil in a heavy pan and fry the cinnamon, cloves, cardamoms, peppercorns and
cumin for 2-3 minutes. Add the rice and stir-fry for 2-3 minutes. Add the boiling water,
reduce the heat, cover and simmer until the rice is nearly tender (20–25 minutes for
white rice, 40–45 minutes for brown rice). Now stir in the nuts and sultanas, re-cover the
pot, and cook until the rice is tender.

PREPARATION TIME 35 MINUTES FOR WHITE RICE,
55 MINUTES FOR BROWN RICE

## Lentil and Brown Rice Pilav

SERVES 4–6

*This is a popular dish throughout the Middle East. It is cheap to make and
provides a healthy combination of foodstuffs. It is usually served topped
with yoghourt and fried onions. The proportion of rice to lentils used is very
much a matter of personal taste. I have used equal amounts of each.*

8 oz (225 g) brown lentils, washed
1¼ pints (700 ml) water
3 medium onions, 1 finely diced and 2 finely sliced
4 fl oz (100 ml) olive or other vegetable oil
8 oz (225 g) long-grain brown rice, washed and drained
salt and black pepper
2 cloves garlic, crushed
½ teaspoon allspice
8 fl oz (225 ml) plain yoghourt

Drain the lentils, put them in a pot with the fresh water, cover and gently boil for 10 minutes. Fry the diced onion golden brown in a quarter of the oil. Stir the fried onion into the lentils, then add the rice and the salt and black pepper to taste. Stir well, bring to the boil, reduce the heat to a simmer, cover the pot, and cook for 40 minutes or until the rice and lentils are tender and all the water has been absorbed. Check the pot towards the end of the cooking period to see that there is enough water to keep the contents moist. Add a little more water if needed. Fry the sliced onions in the remaining oil until dark brown in colour. Stir in the garlic and allspice. Put the rice and lentils in a mound on a serving dish. Make a depression in the top of the mound and pour in the yoghourt. Sprinkle the fried onions and garlic over the top and serve hot or cold.

COOKING TIME 50 MINUTES

*Variations*

Stir 8 oz (225 g) cooked, chopped spinach into the cooked rice and lentils before turning out onto the serving dish.

# Saffron Rice

### SERVES 4

*Saffron rice is an Indian pilav dish. Serve it in place of plain boiled rice with curries or other Indian foods.*

4 oz (100 g) butter or ghee
1 medium onion, thinly sliced
4 whole black peppercorns
4 cloves
1 in (2.5 cm) cinnamon stick
2 cardamoms
8 oz (225 g) long-grain white rice, washed and drained
½ teaspoon turmeric
1 pint (550 ml) water
salt to taste
½ teaspoon saffron strands
2 teaspoons hot water

Heat 3 oz (75 g) of the butter or ghee in a large pot and sauté half the onion until pale gold in colour. Stir in the peppercorns, cloves, cinnamon and cardamoms and sauté with the onions for 2–3 minutes. Add the rice, turmeric and water to the pan, mix well and bring to the boil. Reduce the heat, cover and simmer until the rice is tender (about 12–15 minutes) and the water is absorbed. Towards the end of the cooking time soak the saffron in the hot water (in a saucer or tumbler) and fry the remaining onion golden brown in the rest of the butter or ghee. Turn the cooked rice onto a serving dish and sprinkle the saffron water and the fried onion over the top.

PREPARATION TIME 25 MINUTES

# Couscous

## SERVES 6

*Couscous is the name of a grain product prepared from coarse semolina. It
is also the name of the famous dish containing it as a main constituent.
Couscous is the national dish of the three North African states, Algeria,
Morocco and Tunisia, and is also popular all over the Middle East.
Couscous is an exciting and exotic dish to serve for special occasions and is
much easier to make than it looks. The basic steps in its preparation are as follows:
Make or buy couscous grains. Making couscous grains is a long and
difficult task and we recommend that you purchase a good-quality brand
(not the instant variety). Make or buy harissa. Harissa is a hot pepper
sauce traditionally used in the preparation and serving of couscous. I give a
recipe here but a ready-made hot pepper sauce may be used instead. Prepare
a chicken and vegetable stew. Prepare and steam the couscous grains over
the cooking stew. The couscous grains are never cooked in the sauce. There
is a special pot, called a couscousier, designed to cook the stew and steam
the couscous at the same time. A saucepan with a snug-fitting colander top
is a fine substitute. Finally the couscous grains are piled on a serving dish
and the chicken and vegetables are lifted out of the pan and arranged over
the grains. Some of the cooking broth is poured over the top and the
remainder served in a side bowl with a small dish of harissa. The diners
help themselves to the broth and the hot sauce.*

### Harissa
*1 tablespoon (15 ml) cayenne*
*1 teaspoon ground cumin seeds*
*1 teaspoon caraway seeds*
*1 clove garlic, finely chopped*
*1/2 teaspoon salt*
*2 tablespoons (30 ml) olive oil*

### Couscous
*1 1/2 lb (750 g) couscous*
*1 1/2 pints (900 ml) water*
*4 oz (100 g) butter*
*6 chicken legs or breasts, cut in half*
*2 medium onions, coarsely chopped*
*1/2 teaspoon turmeric*
*1 teaspoon ground ginger*
*1/2 teaspoon cayenne*
*1 teaspoon cinnamon*
*1/2 teaspoon black pepper*
*2 tablespoons (30 ml) chopped parsley or fresh coriander leaves*
*salt*
*8 oz (225 g) chickpeas, soaked overnight and drained, or 20 oz (600 g) tinned
cooked chickpeas, drained*

138

*Water*
*4 medium carrots, scrubbed, cut in half, sliced lengthwise*
*4 small turnips, peeled and quartered (or use potatoes or other root vegetables)*
*4 small courgettes, cut into quarters crosswise*
*2 oz (50 g) pine nuts or almonds or chopped walnuts*
*4 oz (100 g) raisins, soaked in hot water and drained*

To make the harissa, combine the cayenne, cumin, caraway, garlic and salt in a small bowl and mix them together. Pour in the olive oil and stir the mixture into a paste. Transfer the paste to a small pan and cook it with stirring over a low heat for about 5 minutes. Pour the harissa into a small serving bowl and it is ready for use.

Put the couscous grains into a bowl and add the water, slightly salted. Stir well and pour off excess water. Leave the grains to swell, occasionally gently working them with your fingers to break up any lumps and to separate the grains.

Meanwhile melt two thirds of the butter in a large frying pan and brown the chicken pieces on both sides. Transfer the chicken pieces to a large deep pan over which a colander will fit snugly. Add the onions, turmeric, ginger, cayenne, cinnamon, black pepper, parsley or coriander leaves and salt to taste to the chicken. Stir well and gently cook with stirring over a moderate heat for 5 minutes. Add the soaked chickpeas (leave this for later if using tinned chickpeas) and 4 pints (2.3 litres) of water. Bring to the boil, reduce the heat, cover the pan and set to simmer. After 20 minutes, add the carrots and turnips to the pan. Gently stir the mixture, return it to the boil and reduce to a low boil. Leave the pan uncovered.

Turn the couscous grains into the colander and place them over the stew. If steam escapes between the pan and colander, seal the gap with a piece of muslin cloth or foil. Leave the couscous to steam over the stew until the chicken and vegetables are tender (about 50 minutes' total cooking time). Just before this point if you are using tinned chickpeas add them and the courgettes to the pan. Gently stir the mixture, return to the boil and reduce to a low boil. Put the colander back on top of the pan.

Now lightly brown the pine nuts in the remaining butter in a small frying pan, then stir in the raisins and heat through. If you want the stew to be spicy hot, add the harissa to taste. Otherwise serve it in a separate bowl.

As soon as the chicken and vegetables are tender, the couscous is ready to serve. Pile the couscous grains onto a large serving plate. With a slotted spoon remove the chicken and vegetables from the stew and decorate the couscous with them. Moisten the couscous with some of the broth and garnish it with the fried nuts and raisins. Serve with a bowl of the remaining broth and a small side dish of harissa.

PREPARATION TIME 1½ HOURS

# Chakin-Sushi

### SERVES 4 AS A MAIN COURSE, 8 AS A STARTER

*Sushi is a word used to describe a variety of Japanese dishes in which cooked rice, seasoned with vinegar and sugar, is the basic ingredient. In* chakin-sushi *paper thin omelettes are made into pouches in which to wrap the* sushi *rice. The edges of the pouches are secured with fine, coloured string or cotton and then topped with a garnish of cooked shrimps and green peas. Serve one pouch per diner for a very pretty and unusual starter or two each as a main meal.*

### Sushi rice
*12 oz (350 g) white short-grain rice*
*1 pint (550 ml) water*
*4 tablespoons (60 ml) cider or rice wine vinegar*
*3 tablespoons (45 ml) white sugar*
*½ teaspoon salt*

### Omelettes
*4 medium eggs*
*¼ teaspoon salt*
*vegetable oil*

### Garnish
*4 oz (100 g) cooked shrimps*
*2 oz (50 g) cooked green peas*
*1 tablespoon (15 ml) finely chopped parsley*

Wash the rice well by stirring it vigorously in lots of water. Let the rice settle and carefully pour off all the milky residue. Repeat this process until the water remains almost clear (this will be a quick process with good-quality rice; it will take longer with loose-packed rice). Drain the rice and place it in a heavy pan. Add the water, cover the pan and bring quickly to the boil. Turn the heat right down and allow it to simmer for 15 minutes. Turn off the heat and allow the rice to stand for 5 to 10 minutes. Turn the rice into a non-metallic mixing bowl and set aside. Combine the vinegar, sugar and salt and bring the mixture to the boil. Pour this dressing over the hot rice. Stir the rice gently with a wet wooden spoon, while with the other hand fan it with a flat pan lid or rolled-up newspaper. This cools the rice quickly and gives it an authentic shine. Set the rice aside.

To prepare the paper-thin omelettes, beat the eggs with the salt in a mixing bowl. Very lightly coat the bottom of a heavy 8–8 in (20–22 cm) frying pan with oil and heat it until a drop of water evaporates very quickly off the surface. Pour in an eighth of the egg and tilt the pan to spread it evenly and thinly. Cook over a medium heat and turn the omelette over when the top side starts to firm up. Cook the other side for only another few seconds and then slide the omelette onto a large plate. Regrease the pan and repeat the procedure to make eight omelettes.

To assemble the *chakin-sushi*, mould about an eighth of the *sushi* rice into a lightly packed, slightly flattened ball. Place this in the middle of one of the omelettes. Gather the edges of the omelette together and draw to the centre. Fold back the edges, leaving an opening at the top. Tie the pouch into shape by fastening fine, coloured string or cotton under the folds. (Traditionally thin ribbons of toasted nori seaweed are used for this job. They can be obtained from Japanese grocery stores.)

Garnish the top of the rice in each pouch with a few shrimps, peas and a sprinkle of parsley.

Eat the *chakin-sushi* using chopsticks and, if necessary, your fingers. You may wish to provide a sharp knife for those guests who wish to cut open their egg pouches.

PREPARATION TIME 1 HOUR

## *Lentils and Noodles in Butter*
### SERVES 4

*Pasta, perhaps introduced back from Italy many centuries ago, is used in Arab cooking normally in conjunction with rice or lentils or both. Like the Chinese, some Arabs eat long noodles on New Year's Eve as symbols of hoped-for longevity. Serve this lentil and noodle recipe as a side dish to main meals or as a simple main dish.*

8 oz (225 g) brown lentils
salt
8 oz (225 g) thin noodles
4 oz (100 g) butter
2 medium onions, finely diced
$1/2$ teaspoon coriander
$1/4$–$1/2$ teaspoon cayenne
1 teaspoon dried basil
salt and black pepper

Wash and drain the lentils and put them in a heavy pot. Cover with water, add salt to taste and bring to the boil. Reduce the heat, cover, and simmer for 1 hour or until the lentils are just tender. Drain and set aside.

Meanwhile put the noodles in a large pan of salted boiling water and cook, with stirring, until just tender. Drain and reserve.

In a large, heavy frying pan melt half the butter and fry the onions until softened and lightly browned. Stir in the spices and basil and cook for a further 2 minutes. Add the cooked lentils and noodles, mix well, season to taste with salt and black pepper, and heat through. Melt the remaining butter and pour it over the lentils and noodles before serving.

PREPARATION TIME 1 HOUR 15 MINUTES

## Pasta with Green Garlic and Tuna Dressing
SERVES 4

*This is a simple and substantial main-meal salad which is also an excellent way of
using leftover spaghetti, although it is worth making at any time with pasta of all shapes.*

*1½ lb (700 g) lightly oiled, cooked pasta cold or warm*

*Green garlic and tuna dressing*
*2 cloves garlic, peeled*
*4 fl oz (100 ml) olive oil*
*2 tablespoons (30 ml) lemon juice*
*½ large bunch of parsley (about 2 oz/50 g)*
*1 teaspoon prepared English mustard*
*6 oz (175 g) tuna fish*
*salt and black pepper to taste*

To make the dressing put all the ingredients (except a little of the parsley and tuna fish for
garnishing) into a liquidizer and blend until a smooth texture is achieved. Put the pasta
into a mixing bowl and pour the dressing over the top. Toss well, test the seasoning, and
divide between individual bowls. Garnish each with a sprinkling of parsley and a few
shreds of tuna fish.

PREPARATION TIME 20 MINUTES WITH PRECOOKED PASTA,
30 MINUTES WITH UNCOOKED PASTA

## Beans and Pasta in Tomato Sauce
SERVES 4

*An excellent, hearty main meal with a protein-rich combination of beans and pasta.*

*6 oz (175 g) dried haricot beans, soaked overnight*
*½ pint (300 ml) Tomato Sauce (see p.90)*
*6 oz (175 g) small elbow or shell pasta*
*1 tablespoon (15 ml) olive oil*
*1 teaspoon prepared mustard*
*2 tablespoons (30 ml) finely chopped fresh parsley*
*salt and black pepper*
*2 tablespoons (30 ml) cumin seeds, dry-roasted*

Cook the beans in unsalted water until tender (about 1–1½ hours). Meanwhile prepare
the tomato sauce and keep it hot. Before the beans are ready, cook the pasta until it is *al
dente* or just firm to the bite. Pour the pasta into a colander and drain. Drain the beans and
combine with the pasta, olive oil, mustard, tomato sauce and parsley. Season to taste
with salt and black pepper and serve garnished with cumin seeds.

PREPARATION TIME 1½ HOURS
SOAKING TIME 12 HOURS

▼▼▼▼▼▼▼▼▼▼▼▼▼▼▼▼▼▼▼▼▼▼▼▼▼▼▼▼▼▼

# Egg Noodles in Vegetable Stock
### SERVES 4

*This quick and filling dish is popular in South East Asia as a speedy lunchtime meal.*
*The dish usually contains chilli peppers, but they can be left out if you do not enjoy hot food.*

*2 tablespoons (30 ml) vegetable oil*
*1 small onion, sliced*
*2 cloves garlic, crushed*
*2 pints (1.1 litre) vegetable or chicken stock*
*1 in (2.5 cm) root ginger, finely chopped*
*salt and black pepper to taste*
*4 oz (100 g) cabbage leaves, shredded*
*1–2 fresh or dried red chillies, finely chopped (optional)*
*3 oz (75 g) beansprouts, washed*
*4 spring onions, chopped*
*12 oz (350 g) egg noodles*
*dark soya sauce to taste*

### Garnish
*select from:*
*sliced hard-boiled eggs*
*thin strips of omelette*
*tomato wedges*
*chopped celery tops*
*fried onion flakes or rings*

Heat the oil in a large saucepan and add the onion and garlic. Stir-fry until the onion is softened. Add the stock, ginger, salt and black pepper. Bring the mixture to the boil, reduce the heat, cover, and simmer for 15 minutes. Add the cabbage leaves and chillies (if used), increase the heat and bring the mixture to a gentle boil. Add the beansprouts, spring onions and noodles. Loosen the strands of noodles with a fork and stir in soya sauce to taste. Adjust the seasoning and simmer the soup, covered, for 5–7 minutes or until the noodles are cooked. Transfer the contents of the pan to a serving dish and garnish before serving.

PREPARATION TIME 30 MINUTES

### Variation
The method given here is a basic one for hot noodles in stock and the ingredients may be altered to include different vegetables or the addition of pieces of cooked chicken or fish.

# Fried Noodles with Broccoli

SERVES 4

*The method described in this Indonesian recipe is a general one and where I have given
broccoli and celery as ingredients, vegetables such as carrots, beansprouts, Chinese
cabbage, mushrooms and so on may be substituted.*

*8 oz (225 g) noodles*
*3 tablespoons (45 ml) vegetable oil*
*1 medium onion, diced*
*2 cloves garlic, crushed*
*1 in (2.5 cm) root ginger, finely chopped*
*12 oz (350 g) broccoli, chopped*
*3 sticks celery, chopped*
*dark soya sauce to taste*
*4 spring onions, chopped*
*salt and black pepper*
*fresh parsley, finely chopped,* and/or *thin omelette strips to garnish*

Drop the noodles into lots of boiling water and cook them until they are just tender. Drain
them and immediately toss them in 1 tablespoon (15 ml) oil; set them aside. Heat the
remaining oil in a large, heavy frying pan or wok and fry the onion, garlic and ginger until
the onion is softened. Add the broccoli and celery and stir-fry for 2–3 minutes. Add the
noodles and stir-fry over a low heat for 2–3 minutes. Add the soya sauce and spring
onions, season to taste with salt and pepper, and stir-fry for another 1–2 minutes. Serve
the fried noodles in individual bowls or a tureen, and garnish.

PREPARATION TIME 25 MINUTES

*Centre right: Saffron Rice (page 137) Bottom left: Fried Noodles with Broccoli (page 144)*
*Centre left: Chakin-Sushi (page 140) Top left: Saffron*

*Top: Flageolet Beans in Green Olive Oil (page 148)*
*Bottom: Haricot Beans with Tuna Fish (page 152)*

# Beans and Beancurd

In this chapter I use the word 'beans' to include beans, peas and lentils, although the collective names for this group of foods are pulses and legumes. They are a good source of protein, carbohydrate and some vitamins and minerals. Mixed with cooked grains, they make a particularly nutritious combination. Beans, peas and lentils are versatile ingredients and they are used in salads, soups, main dishes, stuffings, purées, sauces, spreads and dips.

Dried beans need to be soaked properly before they are cooked. Details of soaking times and methods are given in Cook's Notes (p. 23). Soaking and cooking dried beans yourself is the most nutritious and flavoursome way to use them, but it is sometimes convenient to use tinned cooked beans for an unexpected meal or to make a small quantity of a particular dip or stuffing. In these instances red beans and chickpeas are the most easily available and perhaps the best. For this reason it is handy to have a couple of tins of each in the store cupboard.

The soyabean product beancurd (see p. 34) has also been included in this chapter. Beancurd, also called tofu, is nowadays fairly easily

available. It is a convenient and versatile food and a good source of protein, carbohydrate and minerals. Beancurd, which is included in other recipes throughout the book, is a particularly useful ingredient in making low-fat dressings for salads; fluffed up with a little honey in a blender, it even makes a tasty dressing for fruit salads. Add beancurd to soups, vegetables and salads for extra body.

# Aigroissade

### SERVES 4-6

*In this dish from Toulon in southern France, chickpeas and a variety of cooked vegetables are combined with aioli. The vegetables may be cold but are more often served warm. The ones given in this recipe are only suggestions. A more traditional assortment would be potatoes, French beans, carrots and artichoke hearts, but you may substitute whatever you like. For a speedy preparation of this dish see the note at the end of the recipe.*

*8 oz (225 g) chickpeas, soaked overnight*
*8 oz (225 g) parsnips, chopped*
*salt*
*8 oz (225 g) small Brussels sprouts*
*8 oz (225 g) French beans, cut in 1 in (2.5 cm) lengths*
*8 oz (225 g) tinned artichoke hearts*
*freshly chopped parsley to garnish*

### Aioli
*4 medium cloves garlic*
*salt*
*1 large egg yolk*
*1 teaspoon Dijon mustard*
*8 fl oz (225 ml) olive oil*
*white pepper*
*juice of 1 lemon*

Soak the chickpeas for 12 hours, then drain them, put them into a heavy saucepan and cover them with cold water. Bring to the boil, reduce the heat, cover the pan and simmer for about 1 hour until tender. Meanwhile put the parsnips in a saucepan containing cold water to cover, add salt, cover the pan and bring to the boil. Reduce the heat and simmer for 30 minutes or until tender.

To make the aioli in the traditional way, in a pestle and mortar crush the garlic with a little salt until smooth. Beat the egg yolk in a bowl and stir in the garlic paste and mustard. Add the oil, drop by drop, beating constantly with a wooden spoon. When the sauce is very thick you can add the oil a little faster, still beating constantly. When all the oil has been added, season to taste with salt and pepper and stir in the lemon juice.

To make the aioli with a blender, put the garlic, salt, egg yolks and mustard into the goblet and, with the machine running, add the oil very slowly to form a thick sauce.

▼▼▼▼▼▼▼▼▼▼▼▼▼▼▼▼▼▼▼▼▼▼▼▼▼▼▼▼▼▼▼▼▼▼▼

Season to taste with salt, pepper and lemon juice.

Cook the Brussels sprouts for 8 minutes and the French beans for about 5 minutes or until tender. Drain the artichoke hearts, reserving the liquid. Chop the hearts, then heat them gently in their liquid.

Drain all the cooked vegetables and the chickpeas, and keep them warm in a large serving bowl. Stir to mix, then pour the aioli over them and gently stir it in. Sprinkle with the chopped parsley and serve at once.

*Note:* For speed 1 lb (450 g) tinned chickpeas may be used. Warm them through before mixing.

PREPARATION TIME 1 HOUR
SOAKING TIME 12 HOURS

▼▼▼▼▼▼▼▼▼▼▼▼▼▼▼▼▼▼▼▼▼▼▼▼▼▼▼▼▼▼▼▼▼

# Bulgar Wheat, Vegetable and Bean Casserole
## SERVES 4

*This casserole contains an excellent combination of complementary food stuffs. Served with a green salad, it constitutes a complete meal. For speed and convenience, use tinned beans or leftover cooked beans.*

8 oz (225 g) bulgar wheat
¾ pint (450 ml) water
1 medium onion, chopped
2 tablespoons (30 ml) vegetable oil
1 carrot, scrubbed and sliced
1 green pepper, seeded and chopped
4 oz (100 g) mushrooms, coarsely chopped
3 tomatoes, scalded, peeled and chopped
1 tablespoon (15 ml) tomato purée
2 tablespoons (30 ml) soya sauce
4 oz (100 g) of a single bean or a bean mix, soaked and cooked until tender, then
drained, or 8 oz (225 g) tinned red beans or chickpeas

Lightly dry-roast the bulgar wheat in a heavy pan, then add the water, cover, and simmer for 15 minutes or until the bulgar is just tender. Remove from the heat.

Preheat the oven to 400° F (200° C, gas mark 6). Sauté the onion in the vegetable oil in an ovenproof pan or casserole dish for 2 minutes. Add the carrot, cover, and cook over a moderate heat until the carrot is softened (about 10 minutes). Add the green pepper and mushrooms and cook for a further 2 minutes. Remove the pan from the heat and stir in the tomatoes, tomato purée and soya sauce, then the bulgar wheat and beans. Bake for 20-30 minutes in the hot oven.

PREPARATION TIME 1 HOUR

▼▼▼▼▼▼▼▼▼▼▼▼▼▼▼▼▼▼▼▼▼▼▼▼▼▼▼▼▼▼▼▼▼▼

# Spaghetti with Brown Lentil Bolognese Sauce
## SERVES 4–6

*7 oz (225 g) brown lentils*
*1 pint (550 ml) water*
*1 bay leaf*
*sea salt and freshly ground black pepper*
*4 tablespoons (60 ml) olive oil*
*2 medium onions, chopped*
*1 clove garlic, finely chopped*
*2 medium carrots, chopped*
*2 sticks of celery, sliced*
*1 tablespoon (15 ml) tomato purée*
*16 fl oz (450 ml) vegetable or chicken stock*
*5 fl oz (150 ml) cider*
*4 oz (100 g) mushrooms, sliced*
*1 medium cooking apple, peeled and grated*
*3 tablespoons (45 ml) chopped parsley*
*about 4 oz (100 g) per serving of spaghetti*
*grated Parmesan cheese to garnish*

Boil the lentils in the water with the bay leaf and seasoning until cooked (about 1 hour). Add more water to the pan as necessary. Heat the olive oil in a large, heavy-bottomed saucepan and cook the onions and garlic until soft. Stir in the carrots and celery and continue cooking until the onions are brown. Add the tomato purée, stock and cider. Bring the mixture to the boil and then add the mushrooms and apple. Cover and simmer for 45 minutes. Add the chopped parsley and more seasoning if necessary.

Cook the spaghetti in the normal way, adding a little oil to prevent it sticking.

Serve either on individual plates or on one large serving dish with the sauce piled in the middle. Sprinkle the top with Parmesan.

PREPARATION TIME 2 HOURS

▼▼▼▼▼▼▼▼▼▼▼▼▼▼▼▼▼▼▼▼▼▼▼▼▼▼▼▼▼▼▼▼▼▼

# Flageolet Beans in Green Olive Oil
## SERVES 4

*This recipe was inspired by feasting in autumn in Tuscany. The green virgin olive oil is important for the dish.*

*6 oz (175 g) dried flageolet beans*
*6 oz (175 g) French beans*
*2 tablespoons (30 ml) extra virgin olive oil*
*juice of 1 lemon*
*sea salt and freshly ground black pepper*
*2 tablespoons (30 ml) parsley, roughly chopped*

Cover the flageolet beans with water and soak for 2 hours. Now cook them in twice their volume of water for 30 minutes until just tender. Meanwhile top and tail and halve the fresh beans. Towards the end of the cooking time for the flageolet beans, cook the fresh beans separately in boiling, lightly salted water for about 3 minutes. Drain both lots of beans and combine them with the olive oil, lemon juice and parsley. Season to taste with salt and black pepper and serve immediately with crusty French bread to mop up the oil.

PREPARATION TIME 35 MINUTES

SOAKING TIME 2 HOURS

## *Falafel with Garlic and Yoghourt Dressing*

SERVES 4

*7 oz (225 g) dried chickpeas, soaked overnight*
*2 fl oz (50 ml) olive oil*
*juice of 1 large lemon*
*6 large cloves garlic, crushed*
*5 fl oz (125 ml) tahini*
*3 tablespoons (45 ml) chopped parsley*
*salt*
*1 egg, beaten*
*2 oz (50 g) wholemeal flour*
*3 oz (75 g) fine sieved wholemeal breadcrumbs*
*sunflower seed oil for shallow frying*
*½ pint (275 ml) natural yoghourt*
*1 tablespoon (15 ml) finely chopped fresh mint (optional)*

Cook the chickpeas in plenty of water until very tender (at least 2 hours). Drain them, reserving the cooking water. Place the chickpeas in a food processor or liquidizer. Add the olive oil, lemon juice, half the garlic, tahini, parsley and salt to taste and blend until smooth. Add some of the cooking water if the mixture is too stiff to blend. You should aim for a fairly stiff consistency. With wet hands, form the mixture into four large or eight small patties and then coat them in beaten egg, flour and breadcrumbs. Shallow-fry the patties until they are pale golden brown, in the sunflower seed oil.

Combine the remaining garlic with the yoghourt, fresh mint (if available) and salt to taste.

Serve the falafel piping hot accompanied by the cold yoghourt sauce.

PREPARATION TIME 20 MINUTES (PLUS 2 HOURS COOKING TIME

FOR THE CHICK PEAS)

SOAKING TIME 12 HOURS

## Chickpea, Butterbean and Tahini Casserole
### SERVES 4

*This casserole is simple to prepare but it is nevertheless very tasty and nutritious.*

2 medium onions, chopped
2 cloves garlic, crushed
2 tablespoons (30 ml) vegetable oil
1 tablespoon (15 ml) tahini
8 oz (225 g) chickpeas, soaked and cooked or 1 lb (450 g) tinned chickpeas, drained
4 oz (100 g) butterbeans, soaked and cooked, or 8 oz (225 g) tinned butter beans,
drained
1 lb (450 g) tomatoes, skinned and chopped
¼ teaspoon grated nutmeg
2 teaspoons chopped fresh basil or 1 teaspoon dried basil
sea salt

Preheat the oven to 350° F (180° C, gas mark 4). Sauté the onions and garlic gently in the oil in a frying pan for 5 minutes. Put them in a casserole dish with the tahini, chickpeas, butterbeans, tomatoes, nutmeg, basil and salt to taste, and mix well. Cover and cook for 45 minutes in the hot oven.

PREPARATION TIME 1 HOUR FOR COOKED BEANS,
2 HOURS FOR UNCOOKED BEANS
SOAKING TIME IF USING DRIED BEANS 12–24 HOURS

## Chinese Fried Vegetables and Mung Beans
### SERVES 4

*The variety of beansprouts we are most familiar with are cultivated from mung beans,
but the beans are good in their own right and also need less soaking and cooking time
than other beans.*

8 oz (225 g) mung beans
1 pint (550 ml) water
2 tablespoons (30 ml) vegetable oil
1 clove garlic, crushed
1 medium onion, sliced
1 medium green pepper, seeded and diced
2 medium courgettes, sliced
4 oz (100 g) mushrooms, sliced
2 teaspoons finely grated root ginger
1 tablespoon honey
2 tablespoons (30 ml) soya sauce
2 teaspoons cornflour

Soak the mung beans in the water for 2-4 hours and then simmer in the same water for 40-45 minutes or until tender. Drain and set the beans aside. Heat the vegetable oil in a heavy frying pan or wok and stir-fry the garlic, onion, green pepper and courgettes until softened. Add the mushrooms and ginger and stir-fry for a further minute. Blend together the honey, soya sauce and cornflour and pour the mixture over the vegetables. Add the mung beans and mix well. Stir and cook for a further 3-4 minutes. Serve over hot boiled rice.

PREPARATION TIME 1 HOUR
SOAKING TIME 2–4 HOURS

## Lentil Cayenne
### SERVES 4

*This is a colourful hotchpotch of browns, reds and greens spiked with cayenne pepper. Serve with bread or rice or other grains. To save on cooking time, the lentils should be soaked for 2-3 hours.*

*1 lb (450 g) brown lentils*
*2 tablespoons (30 ml) olive oil*
*2 cloves garlic, crushed*
*2 medium onions, chopped*
*8 oz (225 g) tinned tomatoes, drained and chopped*
*2 medium green peppers, seeded and chopped*
*1 teaspoon paprika*
*1 teaspoon cayenne (more or less for hotter or cooler)*
*salt and black pepper*
*2–3 tablespoons (45 ml) finely chopped fresh parsley or mint*

Put the lentils in a pan and just cover with water. Cook, covered, until just tender. Add more water as needed: when cooked the lentils should be moist, not sloppy. Heat the oil in another pan and gently brown the garlic and onions. Add the tomatoes, green peppers, paprika and cayenne, stir well and cook for 2–3 minutes. Pour the lentils into the vegetables, season to taste with salt and black pepper, cover the pan, and simmer over a very low light for 10 minutes. Remove from the heat, stir in the parsley or mint, and serve.

PREPARATION TIME 45 MINUTES–1 HOUR

▼▽▼▽▼▽▼▽▼▽▼▽▼▽▼▽▼▽▼▽▼▽▼▽▼▽▼▽▼

## *Haricot Beans with Tuna Fish*
### SERVES 4–6

*Tuna fish is one of those rare foods that taste as good tinned as fresh. A small tin adds*
*flavour to a bean or grain dish and increases its protein content. In this recipe tuna is*
*partnered with haricot beans to good effect.*

*2 tablespoons (30 ml) olive oil*
*2 cloves garlic, crushed*
*1 medium onion, sliced*
*12 oz (350 g) haricot beans, soaked overnight and drained*
*1½ pints (800 ml) water*
*8 oz (225 g) tinned tomatoes, drained and chopped*
*8 oz (225 g) tinned tuna fish, drained and cut into chunks*
*1 tablespoon (15 ml) chopped fresh oregano or 1 teaspoon dried oregano*

Heat the oil in a heavy pot and sauté the garlic and onion until golden. Reserve 1 tablespoon (15 ml) of the mixture as a garnish. Add the beans and water, bring to the boil, reduce the heat, and simmer, covered, until the beans are almost tender (about 1½ hours). Add the tomatoes, tuna fish (reserving a little for the garnish) and dried oregano (if you have fresh, save it for later). Stir well and simmer for a further 15 minutes. Stir in the fresh oregano if used, and transfer to a serving bowl. Combine the reserved diced onion and shredded tuna fish and garnish the dish before serving.

PREPARATION TIME 1½–2 HOURS

▼▽▼▽▼▽▼▽▼▽▼▽▼▽▼▽▼▽▼▽▼▽▼▽▼▽▼▽▼

## *Haricot Bean Goulash*
### SERVES 4–6

*Serve this meatless but nevertheless rich-tasting goulash with spaghetti or noodles or*
*bread and a green salad.*

*4 tablespoons (60 ml) vegetable oil*
*1 clove garlic, crushed*
*2 medium onions, thinly sliced*
*8 oz (225 g) mushrooms, sliced*
*1 tablespoon (15 ml) tomato purée*
*1 lb (450 g) haricot beans, soaked overnight and drained*
*16 fl oz (450 ml) boiling water or vegetable stock*
*2 teaspoons paprika*
*½ teaspoon dry English mustard*
*pinch cayenne*
*1 teaspoon caraway seeds*
*1 bay leaf*
*black pepper*
*salt*

▼ ▼ ▼ ▼ ▼ ▼ ▼ ▼ ▼ ▼ ▼ ▼ ▼ ▼ ▼ ▼ ▼ ▼ ▼ ▼ ▼ ▼ ▼ ▼ ▼ ▼ ▼ ▼ ▼ ▼ ▼ ▼ ▼ ▼ ▼ ▼ ▼

Preheat the oven to 325° F (170° C, gas mark 3). Heat the oil in a heavy casserole dish, add the garlic and the onions, and sauté until golden. Add the remaining ingredients, except for the salt, and mix well. Cover, bring to the boil and transfer to the oven. Bake for 2-3 hours or until the beans are tender. Salt to taste and serve.

PREPARATION TIME 3 HOURS (INCLUDING 2–3 HOURS BAKING TIME)

▼ ▼ ▼ ▼ ▼ ▼ ▼ ▼ ▼ ▼ ▼ ▼ ▼ ▼ ▼ ▼ ▼ ▼ ▼ ▼ ▼ ▼ ▼ ▼ ▼ ▼ ▼ ▼ ▼ ▼ ▼ ▼ ▼ ▼ ▼ ▼ ▼

## Green Lentil and Wholewheat Lasagne

### SERVES 4

*This is a low-fat dish but moist and tasty and enjoyed by vegans, vegetarians and demivegetarians alike.*

*1 large onion, chopped*
*3 cloves garlic, crushed*
*2 tablespoons (30 ml) vegetable oil*
*8 oz (225 g) lentils*
*12 oz (350 g) tinned tomatoes, drained and chopped (reserve the juice)*
*1 pint (0.5 litre) water or stock (including the juice from the tomatoes)*
*1 teaspoon garam masala*
*sea salt to taste*
*6 oz (175 g) wholewheat lasagne*
*4 oz (100 g) hazelnuts, roasted and ground*

Sauté the onion and garlic in the oil in a saucepan for 10 minutes. Stir in the lentils and tomatoes and add the water or stock. Bring to the boil, cover and simmer for 45 minutes. Add the garam masala and sea salt to taste. Remove from the heat. Strain off the liquid and reserve.

Cook the lasagne according to the manufacturer's instructions (or for about 15 minutes) and drain.

Preheat the oven to 400° F (200° C, gas mark 6). Using a greased shallow baking dish, and starting and finishing with the lentil mixture, make layers of lasagne and lentils. Gently pour the reserved liquid over the top. Cover with the ground hazelnuts and bake for 45 minutes in the hot oven.

PREPARATION TIME 2 HOURS

# Red Cooked Beancurd and Cucumber

SERVES 4

*This can be served chilled as a summer dish with cold noodles or a rice salad or as a
winter side dish to add some colour and freshness to a starchy meal.*

*1 medium cucumber, seeded and cut into 2 × ¼ in (5 × 0.5 cm) strips
salt
8 oz (225 g) beancurd, cut into 1 in (2.5 cm) cubes
4 tablespoons (60 ml) sesame seed oil
2 tablespoons (30 ml) soya sauce
1 red pepper, seeded and cut into 2 × ¼ in (5 × 0.5 cm) strips
2 teaspoons grated fresh root ginger
2 teaspoons sugar
4 tablespoons (60 ml) rice or cider vinegar*

Place the cucumber in a colander and sprinkle liberally with salt. Leave to stand for 20
minutes.

In a wok or frying pan fry the beancurd in half the oil, gently browning all sides of the
cubes. Remove the beancurd from the pan and set aside in a bowl. Sprinkle with the soya
sauce and leave to marinate.

Rinse the cucumber under cold running water, drain and pat dry on a tea towel.

Add the remaining oil to the wok or pan and add the cucumber, red pepper and ginger.
Stir-fry over a high heat for 2-3 minutes.

Transfer the contents of the pan to a serving dish. Add the sugar, vinegar, beancurd
and soya sauce. Gently mix together and leave to marinate in the refrigerator for 4 or
more hours.

This dish keeps for up to 3 days in the refrigerator.

PREPARATION TIME 30 MINUTES
CHILLING TIME 4 HOURS OR MORE

# Fried Beancurd

SERVES 4

*Fried beancurd is good both as a snack on its own or with Speedy Chilli Sauce (see p.
93), or with other dishes as part of a meal.*

*4 × 4 oz (100 g) cakes fresh beancurd, cut into 1 in (2.5 cm) cubes
oil for deep-frying
2 tablespoons (30 ml) dark soya sauce
4 spring onions, finely chopped, to garnish*

Heat the oil (about 2 in/5 cm) in a frying pan and deep-fry the beancurd cubes, a portion at a time, until crisp and golden brown on all sides. Remove them from the pan with a slotted spoon, drain them on absorbent kitchen paper and place them on a serving dish. Pour the soya sauce over the cubes, garnish with chopped spring onions and serve.

*Note:* Pressed beancurd is less fragile and easier to fry than the unpressed variety. See p. 34 for pressing method.

PREPARATION TIME 15 MINUTES

## *Fried Beancurd with Vegetables*

SERVES 4

*Ingredients as for Fried Beancurd above, plus:*

*2 fl oz (50 ml) soya sauce*
*3 tablespoons (45 ml) crunchy peanut butter*
*2 cloves garlic*
*1-2 fresh or dried red chillies*
*2 tablespoons (30 ml) lemon juice*
*2 tablespoons (30 ml) water*
*1 teaspoon salt*
*4 oz (100 g) beansprouts*
*4 oz (100 g) cabbage, shredded*
*½ cucumber, peeled, seeded and diced*
*4 spring onions, chopped, to garnish*

Set a large pan of water to boil for later use. Fry the beancurd as in the Fried Beancurd recipe above and keep it warm in a hot oven.

Put the soya sauce, peanut butter, garlic, chillies, lemon juice, water and salt into a blender or food processor and blend the mixture to a smooth consistency.

Remove all but 2 tablespoons (30 ml) of oil from the frying pan in which the beancurd was fried. Add the sauce and stir-fry over a moderate heat for 4-5 minutes. Remove from the heat.

Lightly blanch the beansprouts and cabbage separately in fast-boiling water and drain them.

Put the fried beancurd onto a serving dish, surround it with beansprouts and cabbage, sprinkle with the diced cucumber, cover with the sauce, and garnish with spring onions.

PREPARATION TIME 30 MINUTES

155

▼▼▼▼▼▼▼▼▼▼▼▼▼▼▼▼▼▼▼▼▼▼▼▼▼▼▼▼▼▼▼▼▼▼▼

# Beancurd Burgers
### SERVES 4

*Delicious low-fat burgers. Serve, if you wish, with a sauce (see pp. 89–94).*

*4 tablespoons (60 ml) vegetable oil*
*½ medium onion, finely diced*
*1 small green pepper, seeded and finely diced*
*1 medium carrot, grated*
*12 oz (350 g) beancurd, drained*
*2 tablespoons (30 ml) wholemeal flour*
*1 egg, beaten*
*4 oz (100 g) cheese, grated*
*salt to taste*
*wholemeal flour for dusting*

Heat half the oil in the frying pan and add the onions, green pepper and carrot. Stir-fry until the onion is softened. Mash the beancurd in a mixing bowl and add the fried vegetables, flour, egg, cheese and salt. Mix well and then, with wet hands, form the mixture into about twelve small burger shapes. Dust them with flour and fry them until brown on both sides in the remaining oil.

PREPARATION TIME 25 MINUTES

▼▼▼▼▼▼▼▼▼▼▼▼▼▼▼▼▼▼▼▼▼▼▼▼▼▼▼▼▼▼▼▼▼▼▼

# Honey-Baked Beans
### SERVES 4–6

*Honey-baked beans are a distinct improvement on ordinary tinned baked beans. Serve them with wholemeal bread and a green salad for a nutritious and filling meal. They are also good on their own on toast.*

*1 lb (450 g) haricot beans, soaked overnight and drained*
*2 tablespoons (30 ml) vegetable oil*
*2 medium onions, chopped*
*3 tablespoons (45 ml) honey*
*4 tablespoons (60 ml) tomato purée*
*1 tablespoon (15 ml) French mustard (or other mild mustard)*
*salt to taste*

To prepare the beans, cover them with water in a pot and cook until tender (about 1½ hours). Drain the beans and reserve the liquid. Preheat the oven to 350° F (180° C, gas mark 4). In a casserole dish (about 9-12 in/23-30 cm) in diameter) heat the oil and sauté the onion until softened. Add the drained beans, 8 fl oz (225 ml) of the cooking liquid and the remaining ingredients. Mix well, cover, and cook in the preheated oven for 20 minutes; uncover the dish and cook for a further 20 minutes.

PREPARATION TIME 2½ HOURS (OR 1 HOUR WITH PRECOOKED BEANS)

# EGGS,
# CHEESE AND YOGHOURT

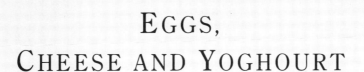

Eggs, cheese and yoghourt are convenient and versatile ingredients and, together with other dairy products, constitute a group of foods that contribute to the protein content of a demivegetarian diet. However, eggs, cheese, butter and, to a lesser extent, milk and yoghourt also contain saturated fats, and they should therefore be eaten in moderation as part of a balanced diet (see Nutrition, p. 9). In Cook's Notes I discuss the low-fat dairy products now available and also give a list and description of the most common varieties of cheese used for culinary purposes.

For instructions on making yoghourt, see p. 29.

## Bulgar Wheat, Egg and Cheese Gratin
SERVES 4

*This recipe offers an unusual method of combining bulgar wheat (or other grains) with eggs and cheese to produce a protein-rich, non-meat meal. The dish may also be made with left-over cooked rice or millet.*

*2 tablespoons (30 ml) vegetable oil*
*2 cloves garlic, crushed*
*1 medium onion, chopped*
*1 green pepper, seeded and diced*
*1 lb (450 g) cooked bulgar wheat (8 oz/225 g uncooked weight)*
*8 oz (225 g) cheese, grated*
*2 eggs, beaten*
*10 fl oz (275 ml) milk*
*1 bunch parsley, finely chopped*
*½ teaspoon dill seeds*
*salt and black pepper to taste*

Preheat the oven to 350° F (180° C, gas mark 4). Sauté the garlic, onion and green pepper in the oil until softened. Combine the mixture with the remaining ingredients and mix well together. Place in a greased baking dish and bake for 35 minutes or until nicely browned.

PREPARATION TIME 50 MINUTES

## Coriander Cream Eggs and Mushrooms
SERVES 4

*A colourful cold salad of boiled eggs and mushrooms in a delicious coriander cream sauce.*

*4 fresh eggs*
*5 oz (150 ml) coriander cream sauce (see p. 92)*
*4 oz (100 g) white mushrooms, stalks trimmed off*
*juice of ½ lemon*
*about 20 black olives*
*4 sprigs coriander to garnish*

Boil the eggs quite hard. Cool them under running water, shell and quarter them. Take four plain white side plates. Place a good heaped tablespoon of the green coriander sauce in the centre of each plate. Arrange the quartered eggs, yellow side up, around this. Finely slice the mushrooms and place them around the eggs. Dress the mushroom slices with lemon juice. Scatter the black olives on the plates and garnish with the coriander sprigs.

PREPARATION TIME 15 MINUTES

# Salade Roquefort

SERVES 4

*Roquefort cheese is extremely expensive but, as the cost of the other ingredients in this
vegetarian dish is low, the extravagance can be justified.*

*2 oz (50 g) butter*
*2 oz (50 g) Roquefort cheese*
*5 fl oz (150 ml) olive oil*
*2 fl oz (50 ml) white wine vinegar*
*1 teaspoon good-quality English mustard*
*½ clove garlic, crushed*
*salt and freshly ground black pepper*
*2 slices wholemeal bread (cut from a small tin loaf)*
*salad ingredients to line four individual bowls to include as many of the
following as available:*
*curly endive*
*iceberg lettuce*
*radicchio*
*chicory*
*watercress*
*3 oz (75 g) walnuts, roughly chopped*

Mash the butter and Roquefort cheese until very smooth. Put the olive oil, vinegar, mustard, garlic and seasoning in a jam jar, seal it tightly and shake vigorously until the ingredients have emulsified. Gradually add this dressing to half the Roquefort butter. (The whole of this operation can be done in a liquidizer.) Arrange the salad ingredients in individual shallow bowls.

Cut the slices of bread into ½ in (1.25 cm) squares. Sauté these gently in the remaining cheese butter.

Arrange the hot croutons on the salad leaves and scatter the walnuts over the top. Pour the dressing onto the salad and season with more black pepper.

PREPARATION TIME 20 MINUTES

▼▼▼▼▼▼▼▼▼▼▼▼▼▼▼▼▼▼▼▼▼▼▼▼▼▼▼▼▼▼▼▼▼▼▼▼▼

# Courgette- and Leek-Stuffed Crêpes
## SERVES 4

*Fromage frais (see p. 30), an ingredient in this recipe, is increasingly available in good supermarkets. Sieved cottage cheese mixed with a little cream can be used instead although the fat content will be higher.*

*12 oz (350 g) courgettes*
*2 medium leeks*
*1 teaspoon sunflower seed oil*
*sea salt and freshly ground black pepper*
*grated zest of ½ lemon*
*9 oz (250 g) fromage frais*
*12 crêpes (see recipe below)*
*2 oz (50 g) Gruyère cheese, grated*
*1 tablespoon (15 ml) grated Parmesan cheese*

Grate the courgettes and finely slice the white parts of the leeks. Smear the bottom of a heavy-bottomed saucepan with the sunflower seed oil. Cook the vegetables very slowly in the covered pan until they start to wilt. Season with the sea salt and black pepper. Add the lemon zest and then, after a minute, remove the pan from the heat and mix in the *fromage frais*. Divide this filling among the crêpes and either fold or roll to contain the stuffing. Arrange in a long ovenproof dish, sprinkle the two cheeses over the top, and gently reheat before serving.

PREPARATION TIME 20 MINUTES

▼▼▼▼▼▼▼▼▼▼▼▼▼▼▼▼▼▼▼▼▼▼▼▼▼▼▼▼▼▼▼▼▼▼▼▼▼

# Spinach and Yoghourt Crêpes
## SERVES 4

*These crêpes are good on their own or with a cheese sauce (see p. 90).*

*4 oz (100 g) wholemeal flour*
*1 egg, beaten*
*10 fl oz (275 ml) milk*
*2 tablespoons (30 ml) vegetable oil*
*1 tablespoon (15 ml) vegetable margarine*
*1½ lb (80 g) fresh spinach, finely chopped*
*4 tablespoons (60 ml) natural yoghourt*
*nutmeg*
*salt and pepper*

Place the flour in a large mixing bowl, make a well in the centre and add the egg. Gradually whisk in half the milk and beat until smooth. Add the remaining milk and 1 tablespoon (15 ml) of oil.

*Top: Roquefort Butter and dressing in jar (page 159) Bottom right: Courgette-and Leek-Stuffed Crêpe (page 160) Bottom left: Salade Roquefort before dressing added (page 159)*

*Top left: Rosehip Tea in infuser. Top Right: Hibiscus Flower Tea. Centre right: Dried Fruit in Hibiscus Tea (page 170) Bottom right: Oranges and Zest (page 170) Bottom left: Sliced Mango with Black Grapes (page 170) Centre left: Mango with Rosehip tea bags*

Heat a 6 in (15 cm) omelette pan and wipe round the inside with a piece of absorbent paper dipped in a little of the remaining oil. Pour in enough batter to coat the base of the pan thinly. Cook until the underside is brown, turn over and cook for another 10 to 15 seconds. Turn out onto greaseproof paper. Repeat with the remaining batter, making twelve pancakes in all. Stack with greaseproof paper in between to prevent them sticking.

Melt the margarine in a saucepan over a low heat. Add the spinach and cook for 5 minutes, stirring occasionally. Remove from the heat and stir in the yoghourt, then season with nutmeg, salt and pepper.

Place a portion of the filling in the centre of each pancake, roll up like a cigar and place under a hot grill to warm through. Serve immediately.

PREPARATION TIME 35 MINUTES

## Gratin of Potatoes and Mushrooms
### SERVES 4

*This is a creamy dish. Serve it with steamed vegetables and a simple salad. For a gratin with a more robust flavour, distribute five or six small anchovies over the first layer of potatoes.*

*2 oz (50 g) butter*
*1 clove garlic, cut in half*
*1 lb (450 g) potatoes, peeled and thinly sliced*
*salt and freshly ground black pepper*
*8 oz (225 g) mushrooms, sliced*
*4 fl oz (100 ml) fresh cream*
*4 fl oz (100 ml) milk*
*6 oz (175 g) mozzarella cheese, sliced*

Preheat oven to 350° F (180° C, gas mark 4). Rub the base and sides of an oval gratin dish with half the butter and the garlic clove. Arrange half the potato slices in the bottom of the dish and season with salt and black pepper. Place the mushroom slices in a layer on top and then the remainder of the potato. Season again. Combine the cream and milk and pour them into the dish. Dot the top of the potatoes with the remaining butter. Cover the top with mozzarella cheese and bake for 1 hour 15 minutes until the potatoes are cooked and the top is golden brown.

PREPARATION TIME 1½ HOURS

## Cheese Enchiladas

SERVES 4–6

*Enchiladas are tortillas (Mexican cornmeal pancakes or flat breads) filled with cheese,*
*cream, chicken, fish or meat stuffing. Here a recipe for a single cheese filling is given,*
*but shredded cooked chicken or fish may be added to the filling or you could make up*
*your own ideas. A simple variation is to use shredded chicken or grated cheese, lettuce*
*leaves and avocado slices.*
*Tortillas are now readily available in specialist food shops, but if you can obtain*
*good cornmeal flour (sometimes called* masa harina *on the pack), they are simple*
*to make at home.*
*The cheese enchiladas can be baked with a cheese topping or in a tomato sauce.*
*Both methods are given.*

### Tortillas (or use 10 shop-bought tortillas)
*4 oz (100 g) 100% wholemeal flour*
*4 oz (100 g) cornmeal flour (*masa harina*)*
*2 oz (50 g) vegetable margarine*
*pinch of salt*
*½ pint (300 ml) hot water*

### Cheese filling
*1 medium onion, finely diced*
*4 tablespoons (60 ml) vegetable oil or melted butter*
*1 lb (450 g) Cheddar cheese, grated*
*2 tablespoons (30 ml) finely chopped parsley*
*¼ teaspoon chilli powder*
*¼ teaspoon ground cumin*
*salt and black pepper to taste*

### Topping
*4 oz (100 g) Cheddar cheese, grated*
*1 pint (550 ml) tomato sauce (see p. 90) (optional)*

To make the tortillas, combine the flour, cornmeal, margarine and salt and mix well to form a coarse meal. Add the hot water slowly to form a firm dough that does not stick to the sides of the bowl. Divide the dough into ten pieces and roll them into balls. Flatten the balls and roll them out on a floured board into rounds about 6 in (15 cm) in diameter. Heat an ungreased frying pan over a moderate flame and cook one or two tortillas at a time. Turn them frequently until they are flecked with brown on both sides. (Cold tortillas may be reheated by the same method.) Remove them to a moderate oven to keep warm while you cook the rest.

To make the enchiladas preheat the oven to 400° F (200° C, gas mark 8). Sauté the onion in half the oil or butter until softened. Combine the onion, oil it has been cooked in, cheese, parsley, chilli powder, cumin and seasoning and mix well together. Place a line of this filling down the centre of each tortilla and fold it over firmly. Place each folded tortilla on a greased baking dish so that it is held in place by the tortillas on each side. Brush the tops with the remaining oil or butter and, if they are to be baked with just a cheese topping, sprinkle the cheese over the top and bake them, uncovered for 15 minutes in the preheated oven. Otherwise pour the tomato sauce over the top, sprinkle with the cheese and bake for 20 minutes.

PREPARATION TIME 30 MINUTES WITH SHOP-BOUGHT TORTILLAS,
45 MINUTES WITH HOMEMADE TORTILLAS

# *Vegetarian Lasagne with Cheese Topping*
## SERVES 6

*This is a dish to serve to friends who think a meal without meat cannot be exciting.*

*1 small aubergine, roughly chopped*
*1 tablespoon (15 ml) vegetable oil*
*1 small onion, finely chopped*
*8 oz (225 g) mushrooms, sliced*
*8 oz (225 g) tinned tomatoes, coarsely chopped*
*2 tablespoons (30 ml) tomato purée*
*½ teaspoon dried basil*
*1 teaspoon dried oregano*
*pinch of brown sugar*
*salt and black pepper*
*12 oz (350 g) ricotta cheese*
*1 egg*
*8 oz (225 g) wholemeal lasagne, cooked and drained*
*6 oz (175 g) mozzarella cheese, grated*
*2 oz (50 g) Parmesan cheese*

Place the chopped aubergine in a sieve or colander, sprinkle well with salt, cover and leave to drain for 30 minutes. Rinse well.

Heat the oil in a saucepan, add the onion and cook over a moderate heat until soft. Add the aubergine and mushrooms and cook for a further 5 minutes. Add the tomatoes, tomato purée, basil, oregano and brown sugar, stir, cover, and simmer for 30 minutes or until thick. Season with salt and black pepper.

Preheat the oven to 350° F (180° C, gas mark 4). In a bowl combine the ricotta cheese and egg and mix well. Spread a third of the aubergine sauce over the base of a baking dish, cover with half the lasagne, then spread the ricotta cheese mixture over the lasagne. Continue in layers with half the mozzarella cheese, a third of the aubergine sauce, the remaining lasagne, the rest of the aubergine sauce, and the rest of the mozzarella cheese. Sprinkle with Parmesan cheese. Bake in the preheated oven for 25 to 30 minutes or until the cheese is golden. Serve immediately.

PREPARATION TIME 1 HOUR

# Bistro's Wholemeal Pizza
### SERVES 4

*Pizzas are excellent demivegetarian foods. They combine the complementary ingredients of grains (in the flour), vegetables (in the sauce), and protein groups such as cheese, fish or chicken in the topping. They are particularly convenient to make if you make your own bread since a portion of the dough can be used to make a pizza. The recipe given here is the one we use in the restaurant of which I am a partner.*

*Dough*
¼ oz (7 g) fresh yeast
1 teaspoon brown sugar
5 fl oz (150 ml) lukewarm water
4 oz (100 g) wholemeal flour
1 teaspoon salt
1 tablespoon (15 ml) vegetable oil

*Pizza Sauce*
2 tablespoons (30 ml) olive oil
1 lb (450 g) ripe tomatoes, peeled and chopped or 14 oz (400 g) canned, peeled
tomatoes, chopped
2 tablespoons (30 ml) tomato purée
2 teaspoons fresh oregano, chopped, or 1 teaspoon dried oregano
salt and pepper

*Pizza Topping*
1 medium onion, thinly sliced
2 oz (50 g) mushrooms, wiped and sliced
1 medium green pepper, cored, seeded and thinly sliced
8 oz (225 g) Cheddar cheese, grated
plus, as an option for the topping;
anchovies
tuna fish, shredded
cooked chicken, shredded

### To make the dough
Cream the yeast and sugar together, add the warm water and set aside in a warm place for 15 to 20 minutes or until the mixture has frothed up. Combine the flour, salt and oil in a mixing bowl, add the yeast mixture and mix into a fairly soft dough which comes away from the sides of the bowl easily. Remove the dough from the bowl and knead on a floured surface for 5 minutes to form a smooth, elastic dough. (Alternatively, place flour, salt and oil into the bowl of a food processor and, with the machine running, pour the yeast liquid through the feed tube, process until the mixture forms a ball around the knife and then for another 15 to 20 seconds to knead the dough.) Place the dough in a clean bowl and cover with a damp cloth; leave in a warm place for 45 minutes to 1 hour.

*To make the pizza sauce*

Heat the oil in a saucepan, add the tomatoes, tomato purée, half the oregano, salt and pepper. Cook over a low heat, stirring occasionally, for 15 minutes or until the excess liquid has evaporated and you are left with a thick purée. Cool. Preheat the oven to 475°F (240°C, gas mark 9).

*Finally*

Punch down the dough with your fists and knead lightly until smooth again. Grease the base of a pizza tray or flan ring. Roll the dough over the base, keeping the centre ⅛ in (2.5 cm) thick. Spread the pizza sauce evenly over the pizza dough, but leaving the edges uncovered. Place the onion on top followed by the mushroom, pepper, cheese and anchovies, and the tuna or chicken if used. Finally, sprinkle with the remaining oregano. Bake the pizza in the preheated oven for 10 minutes or until the cheese is golden brown.

PREPARATION TIME (INCLUDING 1 HOUR 45 MINUTES DOUGH PROVING)
2½ HOURS

## Quick Pizza Sandwich
MAKE ONE PER PERSON

*One baked pitta bread per person*
*tomatoes, sliced*
*cheese, grated*
*salt and freshly ground black pepper*
*olives*
*oregano*

Preheat the oven to 450°F (230°C, gas mark 8). Cut a pitta bread around the circumference so that you can open it up as two circles joined by a hinge of bread. Layer one side with tomato slices, cover with the grated cheese and season with salt and black pepper. Decorate with olives, sprinkle on oregano and then fold the empty half of the bread over the top. Prepare one pizza sandwich per person and then bake them in the hot oven for 5 minutes or until the cheese has melted.

PREPARATION TIME 15 MINUTES

# Stuffed Tomatoes and Cheese and Nut Balls
## SERVES 4

*The following two recipes are good individually or together. Served alone, the stuffed tomatoes make an unusual accompaniment to a main dish of grains and a sauce, or they could be served with salad and bread as a light meal. The cheese and nut balls are good in a tomato sauce with spaghetti. Alternatively, prepare the two dishes at the same time and bake them together in the same oven. Served with a simple green salad and bread, they are excellent.*

### Tomatoes with walnut and cottage cheese filling
4 large firm tomatoes
salt and black pepper to taste
4 oz (100 g) cottage cheese
2 oz (50 g) chopped walnuts
2 oz (50 g) wholemeal breadcrumbs
1 tablespoon (15 ml) freshly diced onion
½ teaspoon dried thyme
1 tablespoon (15 ml) vegetable oil

Preheat the oven to 350° F (180° C, gas mark 4). Cut the tops off the tomatoes and scoop out the seeds, leaving a ½ in (1 cm) thick shell. Sprinkle the inside of each shell with a little salt and black pepper. Combine the cottage cheese, walnuts, breadcrumbs, onion, thyme, salt and black pepper and mix well. Stuff the tomatoes with the mixture and press the tops back into place. Brush the tomatoes with oil and put them on a greased baking sheet. Bake in the preheated oven for 30-35 minutes.

### Cheese and nut balls
1 medium onion, finely diced
2 cloves garlic, crushed
2 tablespoons (30 ml) vegetable oil
8 oz (225 g) ground mixed nuts
8 oz (225 g) wholemeal breadcrumbs
4 oz (100 g) cheese, grated
2 teaspoons soya sauce
black pepper to taste
2 eggs, beaten

Sauté the onion and garlic in the oil until softened. Remove them from the heat and stir in the ground nuts and the breadcrumbs. Combine the cheese, soya sauce, pepper and beaten eggs and mix well. Stir the nut and cheese mixtures together and mix thoroughly. Preheat the oven to 350° F (180° C, gas mark 4). With wet hands form the mixture into 2 in (5 cm) balls and place them on a greased baking sheet. Bake for 10-12 minutes on one side, then turn them over and bake for a further 10-12 minutes or until brown and firm.

PREPARATION TIME 1 HOUR

## Stilton Cheese with Fresh Pineapple and Honeydew Melon Salad
### SERVES 4

*This is a delightful last course for a dinner party or a refreshing light meal.*

*½ small pineapple, peeled and cut into small cubes*
*½ small melon, peeled and cut into small cubes*
*juice of 1 lime or lemon*
*Stilton cheese*
*water biscuits*

Combine the pineapple and melon and sprinkle with lime or lemon juice. Chill before serving with the cheese and water biscuits. To reduce the preparation time, use the pineapple and melon straight from the fridge.

PREPARATION TIME 15 MINUTES
CHILLING TIME 30 MINUTES

## Baked Fish Omelette and Ginger Lemon Sauce
### SERVES 4 AS A LIGHT MEAL OR STARTER

*An oriental-inspired dish in which fish and eggs are beaten together, baked in the oven and served with a grated ginger and lemon sauce. This omelette is simple to make, economical and good hot or cold. Serve it cold in the summer with salad or in colder months serve it hot with baked potatoes and a green salad.*

*6 oz (175 g) fillet of white fish*
*2 tablespoons (30 ml) soya sauce*
*1 teaspoon honey*
*4 large eggs*
*2 teaspoons vegetable oil*
*juice of 1 lemon*
*2 teaspoons finely grated fresh root ginger*
*sprigs of parsley to garnish*

Preheat oven to 300° F (150° C, gas mark 2). Put the fish, soya sauce, honey and eggs into a liquidizer and purée gently to blend together but leave some shreds of fish intact. Brush an 8 in (20 cm) square shallow baking dish with the oil and pour in the omelette mixture. Bake uncovered until the egg is set and the top is golden brown (about 40 minutes). Run a sharp knife around the omelette edge and lift it out. Divide into four portions. Whisk the lemon juice and grated ginger together and spoon some of the sauce over each omelette portion. Garnish with a sprig of parsley and serve.

PREPARATION TIME 50–60 MINUTES

# *Bombay Eggs*

SERVES 6 AS A SNACK, 3 AS A MAIN MEAL

*Hard-boiled eggs wrapped in a lentil coating and deep-fried, Bombay eggs are rich in
protein. Serve one per person with bread and pickles as a snack or two per person with a
salad as a main dish.*

*2 large onions, diced*
*8 oz (225 g) brown lentils*
*2 tablespoons (30 ml) vegetable oil*
*2 tablespoons (30 ml) grated Cheddar cheese*
*2 tablespoons (30 ml) finely chopped fresh coriander leaves or parsley*
*1-2 teaspoons curry powder to taste*
*1 teaspoon turmeric*
*salt and black pepper to taste*
*6 hard-boiled eggs, shelled*
*plain flour for dusting*
*2 eggs, beaten*
*wholemeal breadcrumbs for coating*
*oil for deep-frying*

Put the onions and lentils in a large pan and mix well together. Cover them well with
water, bring it to the boil and simmer for 1-1½ hours or until the lentils are very soft.
Drain well, reserving the liquid for soup making. Heat the oil in a frying pan, add the
onions and lentils, stir continuously over a low heat until all the moisture has evaporated
and you are left with a fairly thick mixture. Add the cheese, coriander, curry powder,
turmeric, salt and pepper, and mix well. Cool.

Now divide the mixture into six equal portions and use each portion to coat one egg
completely. Dust the coated eggs with seasoned flour, dip each into the beaten egg and
then roll in breadcrumbs. Heat the oil for deep-frying until it just starts to smoke.
Deep-fry the coated eggs three at a time until the outsides are crisp and golden.

PREPARATION TIME 2 HOURS
(INCLUDING 1½ HOURS TO COOK THE LENTILS)

# FRUIT FOR DESSERT
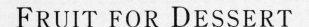

There is nothing to surpass fresh fruit as a healthy dessert. Even if you were to eat all your fruit in its natural state you would take a long time to get bored with it. What could be more inviting on an early summer day than a bowl of glistening, just washed cherries or, on a hot day in late summer, a great red and green wedge of chilled watermelon? You can cube the watermelon and pile it high on a white plate in the centre of the table for people to pick up with forks. What could be simpler or more refreshing after a full meal? Fresh seasonal fruit can provide you with endless trouble-free economical desserts.

Don't forget that there are plenty of fruits to have as treats. Try fresh lychees around Christmas time or, in early spring, when there is little else around to brighten up your day, delicious golden slices of fibreless mango.

## *Fruit Enhances Fruit*

Fruit may be the ultimate convenience dessert but we can always dress it up a little to give a sense of occasion. To improve the flavour, sprinkle lemon juice over ripe melon or squeeze an orange over your strawberries instead of using cream.

Here are some more ideas:

Peel, pith and slice oranges, arrange them in a shallow bowl and dress with the zest and juice of a lemon. You might add a slight sprinkling of sugar or a dribble of honey.

Lay a string of redcurrants across a slice of honeydew melon.

Fill the cavity in a small canteloupe, galia or charentais melon with a little mound of raspberries.

Place a few black grapes alongside a fan of orange mango slices set on a white plate.

Strawberries look wonderful when set alongside peeled and sliced kiwi fruit.

Buy two different coloured melons, cube and mix the flesh together and serve chilled. Try this salad sprinkled with a little finely chopped preserved ginger.

## *Fruit in Liquids*

Ripe peaches served peeled and sliced in a glass of white wine are wonderful. You can dilute the wine with mineral water if you wish.

Dried fruit salads (figs, apricots, peaches, prunes) are delicious if the fruit has been plumped in strong herbal tea rather than in water. Hibiscus-based teas are particularly successful. Pour the freshly made tea over the fruit, allow to cool, chill slightly, and it is ready to serve. Add a few pieces of fresh orange, apple or pineapple if you want to make your fruit salad more colourful.

Fresh fruit salads retain their looks longer if at least one of the fruits is acidic, for example, pineapple. Failing that, add enough orange juice just to cover the fruit.

## *Fruit Sauces*

Sauces are simply made from cherries, raspberries, mangoes, blackcurrants and ripe apricots. Place the fruit in a liquidizer or food processor, add a little honey or other sweetener and perhaps a few drops of lemon juice, and blend till smooth. The sauce is complete. Sauces can be thickened by dissolving a tiny amount of setting agent in a small portion of the sauce gently heated. Stir this well before returning it to the rest of the sauce. Take care not to overthicken these sauces. Do not use cornflour to thicken them as it will mask their clarity and flavour.

Fruit sauces have a multitude of uses:

1   Over other fruit: raspberry sauce over peaches, blackcurrant sauce over poached pears.
2   Served over or alongside a little mound of cottage cheese or *fromage frais.*
3   Poured into a straight-sided glass and topped with yoghourt.
4   Poured over sponge cake or pudding.
5   Used with a dairy product as a topping or a filling for sweet pancakes.
6   Poured over ice cream.
7   Thickened with egg yolks, strained and set with gelatine to make mousses.
8   Mixed with yoghourt and frozen to form sorbets.
9   Stirred and frozen to make water ices.
10  Folded into thick yoghourt and whipped cream and chilled to produce a fool.

## Stuffed Fruit

Fruit large or small, fresh or dried can be stuffed to produce everything in size from a substantial pudding to a petit four. Here are some ideas.

*Stuffed apples:* ringed to stop them bursting, the core cavity stuffed with nuts or dried fruit. Serve with hot apricot sauce.

*Stuffed pears:* halved and cored and filled with nut-flavoured Greek yoghourt.

*Stuffed peaches:* halved and filled with almond crumble, then baked.

*Stuffed prunes:* pitted prunes, plumped in herbal tea, slit and stuffed with walnut halves.

*Stuffed dates:* fresh dates split, the stones removed, the centres filled with spiced soft cheese.

## Baked or Barbecued Fruit

Hot fruit? Try cooking foil-wrapped fruit in the oven or outside over a barbecue. Here are two to start you off:

*Pineapple:* cut vertically into 6-8 wedges in such a way that each piece has its own green tuft of leaves. Place each wedge on a double piece of baking foil, smear with honey, add a teaspoonful of dark rum and seal securely. Cook for 20 minutes or until the fruit is well baked through.

*Banana:* part peel the banana and spread the honey and rum between the flesh and the skin before sealing the fruit tightly in foil. Cook as above.

*Grilled grapefruit:* you can quickly prepare another hot fruit dessert by placing pink grapefruit halves spread with thick honey under a very hot grill until the honey caramelizes.

# CONVERSION TABLES

## Weights and Measures

| Weights | | | Liquids | |
|---|---|---|---|---|
| *Imperial* | *Approximate metric equivalent* | | *Imperial* | *Approximate metric equivalent* |
| ½oz | 15g | | ¼teaspoon | 1.25ml |
| 1oz | 25g | | ½teaspoon | 2.5ml |
| 2oz | 50g | | 1teaspoon | 5ml |
| 3oz | 75g | | 2teaspoons | 10ml |
| 4oz | 100g | | 1tablespoon | 15ml |
| 5oz | 150g | | 2tablespoons | 30ml |
| 6oz | 175g | | 3tablespoons | 45ml |
| 7oz | 200g | | 1fl oz | 25ml |
| 8oz | 225g | | 2fl oz | 50ml |
| 9oz | 250g | | 3fl oz | 75ml |
| 10oz | 275g | | 4fl oz | 100ml |
| 11oz | 300g | | 5fl oz (¼ pint) | 150ml |
| 12oz | 350g | | 6fl oz | 175ml |
| 13oz | 375g | | 7fl oz | 200ml |
| 14oz | 400g | | 8fl oz | 225ml |
| 15oz | 425g | | 9fl oz | 250ml |
| 1lb | 450g | | 10fl oz (½ pint) | 275ml |
| 2lb | 900g | | 15fl oz (¾ pint) | 450ml |
| 3lb | 1.4kg | | 20fl oz (1 pint) | 550ml |
| | 1¾pints | | 1litre | |
| | 2pints | | 1.1litres | |

*Exact conversion:* 1 oz = 28.35 g

172

# British and American Equivalents

This book was written for a British readership. To help the American cook with the system of measurement used, here is a conversion table showing imperial weights with their American cup equivalent.

| British | American |
|---|---|
| 8 fl oz | 1 cup |
| ½ pint/10 fl oz | 1¼ cups |
| 16 fl oz | 1 pint |
| 1 pint/20 fl oz | 2½ cups |
| 2 pints/40 fl oz | 5 cups |
| 2 tablespoons | ⅛ cup/ 1½ tablespoons |
| 8 tablespoons | ½ cup |
| 4 oz ground almonds | 1 cup |
| 5 oz almonds, unblanched | 1 cup |
| 4½ oz dried apricots | 1 cup |
| 7 oz aubergines, diced | 1 cup |
| 6 oz bamboo shoots, drained and sliced | 1 cup |
| 4 oz beancurd, drained | 1 cup |
| 6 oz beans (canned) | 1 cup |
| 3 oz beansprouts | 1 cup |
| 3½ oz broccoli (fresh), sliced | 1 cup |
| 4 oz bulgar wheat | 1 cup |
| 4 oz butter | 1 stick |
| 8 oz butter | 1 cup |
| 4 oz cabbage, shredded, firmly packed | 1 cup |
| 4 oz cauliflower, in florets | 1 cup |
| 4 oz cheese, grated | 1 cup |
| 4 oz cooked chickpeas | 1 cup |
| 2 oz flaked, unsweetened coconut | 1 cup |
| 3½ oz coriander seeds | 1 cup |
| 4 oz sweetcorn kernels | 1 cup |
| 6 oz cornflour | 1 cup |
| 5 oz courgettes, sliced | 1 cup |
| 3½ oz cumin seeds | 1 cup |

| British | American |
|---|---|
| 8 oz cooking dates | 1 cup |
| 4½ oz wholewheat flour | 1 cup |
| 4 oz white flour | 1 cup |
| 4 oz green beans, chopped | 1 cup |
| 7 oz dried lentils | 1 cup |
| 7 oz cooked lentils | 1 cup |
| 3½ oz mangetout | 1 cup |
| 9 oz miso (Japanese soya-bean paste) | 1 cup |
| 2 oz broken noodles | 1 cup |
| 6 oz diced onion | 1 cup |
| 2 oz parsley, finely chopped | 1 cup |
| 6 oz peanut butter | 1 cup |
| 5 oz peanuts | 1 cup |
| 3½ oz black peppercorns | 1 cup |
| 6 oz canned pineapple chunks, drained | 1 cup |
| 6 oz raisins or sultanas | 1 cup |
| 8 oz dry rice (brown or white) | 1¼ cups |
| 6 oz sesame seeds | 1 cup |
| 8 oz cooked spinach | 1¼ cups |
| 1 lb raw spinach | 5 cups |
| 6½ oz cooked red beans | 1 cup |
| 8 oz granulated sugar | 1 cup |
| 6 oz brown sugar | 1 cup |
| 9 oz canned tomatoes | 1 cup |
| 8 oz tomatoes | 2 medium tomatoes |
| 9 oz tomato paste | 1 cup |
| 7 oz vegetable fat | 1 cup |
| 4 oz walnuts, chopped | 1 cup |
| 6½ oz water chestnuts, drained | 1 cup |
| 1 oz yeast | 1 cup |

## Oven Temperatures

| °F | °C | Gas mark |
|-----|-----|-----|
| 225 | 110 | ¼ |
| 250 | 130 | ½ |
| 275 | 140 | 1 |
| 300 | 150 | 2 |
| 325 | 170 | 3 |
| 350 | 180 | 4 |
| 375 | 190 | 5 |
| 400 | 200 | 6 |
| 425 | 220 | 7 |
| 450 | 230 | 8 |
| 475 | 240 | 9 |

# INDEX

EDUCATION